ANCHORED BY LOVE

Anchored by Love

A Family's Journey Through Obstacles, Success, and Reunion

Marie-Claire Moriah Wright

David Saccoh Wright

CONTENTS

PART TWO
CLARA'S JOURNEY

PART FOUR
MAX AND ASH- A JOURNEY TO
RESTAURANT SUCCESS

PART FIVE
FAMILY REUNION CRUISE – A STORY OF CONNECTION AND LOVE

INTRODUCTION

Asher and Charlotte's story began in the halls of their high school, where fate brought together two seemingly different souls. Asher, with his charming smile and reputation as a heartbreaker, was known for his carefree ways and a string of fleeting romances. But when he met Charlotte, everything changed. Charlotte was different—kind, intelligent, and unafraid to see through Asher's facade to the kind heart that lay beneath. Their connection was immediate, and despite Asher's past, their love flourished, defying the expectations of those around them. Charlotte saw in Asher what others did not: the potential for deep love, loyalty, and transformation.

Their love story blossomed into a lifelong commitment, and together they built a beautiful family. They were blessed with three children: Clara, their eldest, who was artistic and introspective; and the twins, Max and Ash, who were outgoing and charismatic, much like their father had been. The twins shared an unbreakable bond and a love for adventure, while Clara often found solace in her own world of books and creativity.

However, as the twins grew more popular, Clara began to feel increasingly overshadowed. The turning point came during Max and Ash's 16th birthday party when a thoughtless prank by her brothers left Clara humiliated and heartbroken. They revealed a cherished baby blanket to their friends, an act meant as a joke but one that deeply embarrassed Clara. The incident triggered a period of depression for Clara, a time when she felt isolated and alone, struggling to find her place in the world.

But Clara's story is one of resilience and strength. She channeled her pain into purpose, dedicating herself to her studies and eventually becoming an accomplished therapist and writer. Clara used her own experiences of overcoming adversity to inspire others, helping her clients navigate their own challenges. Her work wasn't limited to the therapy room; she also gave back to her community through outreach programs designed to foster healing and connection, particularly for those who felt marginalized or misunderstood.

Meanwhile, Max and Ash found their own paths to success. Their love for cooking, which began during family gatherings, blossomed into a shared dream of opening their own restaurant. Max pursued culinary arts with passion, becoming an acclaimed chef known for his innovative dishes. Ash, ever the business-minded twin, excelled in hospitality management, ensuring that their restaurant empire not only thrived but became a beloved part of the community. Together, they built a legacy of culinary excellence, all while finding ways to give back—creating scholarships, organizing charity events, and supporting local causes close to their hearts.

As their children grew and pursued their dreams, Asher and Charlotte watched with pride, knowing that the love and values they had instilled were guiding them. But as time passed and life became busier, they sensed that the family was drifting apart, each member absorbed in their own world. Charlotte, ever the heart of the family, knew it was time to bring everyone back together.

And so, Charlotte and Asher organized a cruise—an adventure designed to reconnect their family and create new memories to cherish. The journey took them to beautiful island destinations, each offering its own unique experiences. In San Juan, Puerto Rico, they snorkeled among vibrant coral reefs; in Punta Cana, Dominican Republic, they explored hidden lagoons; and in Oranjestad, Aruba, they hiked through desert landscapes. Each day brought new adventures—snorkeling in Curacao, hiking in Bonaire, savoring fresh seafood in St. Lucia, and watching the sunsets in St. Kitts.

The cruise was more than just a vacation; it was a journey of reconnection, a time for the family to laugh, bond, and reflect on the love that had always held them together. By the end of the trip, the family had grown closer, forging a bond of love and joy that would carry them through the years to come. The memories they created on the open seas became a lasting testament to the power of family, love, and the unbreakable connection that started with Asher and Charlotte all those years ago.

Their story is a reminder that no matter where life takes you, the anchor of family will always bring you back to what truly matters: love, connection, and the joy of being together.

PART ONE
THE
HEARTBREAKER

CHAPTER 1
THE FIRST CRUSH

INTRODUCTION TO ASHER AND AMANDA

Asher: The Kind, Shy, and Artistic Boy

Asher Kingsley was the kind of boy who often went unnoticed in the hustle and bustle of middle school. He was a slender, quiet 12-year-old with a mop of unruly brown hair that perpetually fell into his gentle, green eyes. While his peers were obsessed with sports and video games, Asher found solace in the pages of his sketchbook. Drawing was his refuge, a way to escape the noise and confusion of adolescence. His artistic talent was evident in the intricate drawings that filled his sketchbook – landscapes, fantastical creatures, and portraits of people he observed from afar. Asher's kind-hearted nature made him a favorite among teachers but largely invisible to his classmates.

Amanda: The Beautiful and Popular Classmate

Amanda Sinclair, on the other hand, was the epitome of popularity. Tall for her age, with flowing blonde hair and bright blue eyes, she had a radiant smile that seemed to light up the room. Amanda excelled in academics, sports, and social activities, effortlessly balancing her responsibilities while remaining approachable and kind. She was the captain of the soccer team, a straight-A student, and the girl everyone wanted to be friends with. Her charm and beauty made her the center of attention, and it was no surprise that many boys in school harbored secret crushes on her – including Asher.

Asher's Admiration for Amanda

Asher's infatuation with Amanda began the moment he first saw her. It was the beginning of sixth grade, and Amanda had just transferred to his school. She entered the classroom with an air of confidence that immediately drew Asher's attention. From then on, he watched her from a distance, marveling at her grace and poise. Asher's feelings for Amanda were pure and innocent. He admired her not just for her looks, but for her kindness and the way she treated everyone with respect, regardless of their social status.

Innocent Attempts to Get Her Attention

Asher's shyness prevented him from approaching Amanda directly, so he found subtle ways to catch her attention. He would leave small drawings on her desk when no one was looking – sketches of flowers, animals, and occasionally, a portrait of her. Amanda often found these drawings and would smile, wondering who the mysterious artist was. Asher also tried to position himself near her in group activities, hoping for a chance to interact with her. He would muster all his courage to say a simple "hi" or offer to help her with a project, his heart racing each time she acknowledged him with a friendly smile or a "thank you."

ASHER'S HEARTBREAK

The Courage to Confess

Asher's admiration for Amanda grew with each passing day, and he finally decided that he had to tell her how he felt. He spent weeks rehearsing what he would say, his stomach knotting with a mix of excitement and fear. One afternoon, after school, Asher saw Amanda sitting alone in the schoolyard, reading a book. It was the perfect opportunity. He took a deep breath, clutched a small, hand-drawn card he had made for her, and walked over to where she sat.

Amanda's Polite but Firm Rejection

Asher's hands trembled as he handed Amanda the card, his voice barely above a whisper. "Amanda, I... I really like you," he stammered, his cheeks flushing. Amanda looked up from her book, surprise and then gentle understanding in her eyes. She took the card and opened it, admiring the beautiful drawing inside. "This is really sweet, Asher," she said softly. "But... I just don't feel the same way." She spoke with kindness, but her words were like daggers to Asher's heart. He forced a smile and nodded, trying to hide the tears that threatened to spill over. "It's okay," he managed to say before quickly turning and walking away, his vision blurred by tears.

The Impact on Young Asher

The rejection left Asher devastated. He had poured his heart into that confession, only to have it handed back to him, untouched. For days, he withdrew into himself, his sketchbook lying forgotten at the bottom of his backpack. The once lively and kind-hearted boy became quiet and introspective, questioning his self-worth and wondering why he wasn't good enough for Amanda. This heartbreak planted a seed in Asher – a seed of doubt and insecurity that would shape his future interactions with others.

Asher's young mind began to form a protective shell around his heart, vowing never to let himself be so vulnerable again. He started to view his sensitivity as a weakness, something that needed to be hidden to avoid further pain. This early heartbreak set the stage for Asher's transformation in the coming years, as he struggled to navigate the complexities of love and relationships, often choosing a path that led to further heartache for himself and others.

Reflection

In the quiet moments of reflection, Asher often thought back to that day in the schoolyard. Amanda's rejection had been a turning point in his life, a painful lesson in the unpredictability of love. It was a memory that stayed with him, a reminder of the vulnerability of the human heart and the fragile nature of youthful crushes. As he grew older, Asher came to understand that heartbreak is an inevitable part of life, but it would take many more experiences for him to fully grasp the importance of resilience, self-worth, and genuine connection. This chapter sets the stage for Asher's journey, highlighting the innocence of first love and the profound impact of early heartbreak on his character development.

CHAPTER 2
THE HEARTBREAK

ASHER'S TRANSFORMATION

From Heartbroken Boy to Confident, Rebellious Teenager

The heartbreak Asher experienced from Amanda's rejection marked the beginning of a significant transformation. Over the next few years, the once shy and kind-hearted boy began to change. He entered high school with a new resolve, determined to never let anyone see his vulnerability again. Asher's appearance evolved along with his attitude. He traded his unkempt hair for a more stylish cut, started working out, and began dressing in trendier clothes. The transformation was more than skin-deep; it was a complete overhaul of his personality.

Asher's newfound confidence was palpable. He walked the halls with an air of self-assuredness, his green eyes now sparkling with a mischievous glint. He became more outgoing, effortlessly blending into different social circles and gaining a reputation as someone who was fun to be around. However, beneath this confident exterior was a rebellious streak. Asher began to defy authority, challenging teachers and skipping classes. His rebellion was a facade, a way to mask the lingering pain of his past heartbreak and the fear of being hurt again.

The Decision to Never Be Vulnerable Again

The most profound change in Asher was his emotional armor. The pain of Amanda's rejection had left a lasting scar, one that he vowed never to reopen. He decided that the best way to protect himself was to keep his emotions locked away. Asher adopted a philosophy of detachment, convincing himself that caring too much was a weakness. This decision led him down a path where genuine connection was replaced with superficial relationships.

Asher's transformation was complete when he made a promise to himself: never again would he allow anyone to have the power to hurt him. This resolve became the driving force behind his actions, influencing how he interacted with others, particularly girls.

JOURNEY AS A PLAYER

A New Lifestyle

Asher's new lifestyle revolved around dating multiple girls with no intention of forming lasting relationships. He quickly gained a reputation as a heartbreaker, someone who was charming and irresistible but ultimately unattainable. His dating strategy was simple: make each girl feel special, but never let them get too close. Asher became adept at playing the game, using his charm and good looks to his advantage. He was always surrounded by admirers, enjoying the attention and the thrill of the chase.

Manipulative Tactics

Asher's tactics were calculated and manipulative. He would shower a girl with compliments, give her his undivided attention, and make her feel like she was the only one in his world. He knew how to read people, identifying their insecurities and desires, and he used this knowledge to his advantage. Asher would often start with small gestures – a handwritten note, a favorite snack, or a thoughtful comment.

These actions would make the girl feel seen and appreciated, drawing her closer to him.

Once he had her interest, Asher would escalate his efforts. He would take her on romantic dates, share personal stories (though never too personal), and create an illusion of intimacy. The girls he dated felt special, believing that they had a genuine connection with him. However, as soon as they began to expect more from the relationship or showed signs of becoming too attached, Asher would start to distance himself. He would become less available, stop responding to messages, and ultimately, break things off with a vague explanation, leaving the girl confused and hurt.

Consequences on the Girls He Dates

The consequences of Asher's actions were far-reaching. Many of the girls he dated were left heartbroken, their self-esteem shattered. They often questioned what they had done wrong and why they weren't enough to keep Asher's interest. Some of them developed trust issues, wary of future relationships and hesitant to open up to others. The emotional toll was significant, and while Asher was aware of the pain he caused, he justified his actions by telling himself that it was better this way – better for him to stay protected and detached.

Glimpses of Internal Conflict and Occasional Guilt

Despite his outward confidence and seemingly care-free attitude, Asher was not immune to moments of internal conflict and guilt. Late at night, when the distractions of the day faded away, he often found himself reflecting on his actions. He would think about the girls he had hurt, replaying the moments of their relationships in his mind. Asher knew that what he was doing was wrong, that his manipulative tactics were causing real pain. But the fear of vulnerability and rejection was stronger than his conscience.

There were times when Asher felt a pang of regret, especially when he saw the hurt in a girl's eyes as he walked away. He would momentarily consider changing his ways, but the walls he had built around his heart were too high to easily tear down. Asher's guilt was fleeting, quickly buried under layers of self-preservation and rationalization. He convinced himself that this was the only way to live, the only way to protect himself from the heartbreak he had experienced as a boy.

Reflection

Asher's journey as a player was marked by a series of superficial victories and deep, unresolved pain. His transformation from a heartbroken boy to a confident, rebellious teenager was driven by a fear of vulnerability, a fear that dictated his every move. The lifestyle he chose brought temporary satisfaction but left a trail of emotional wreckage in its wake. Asher's story was one of internal struggle, where the battle between his desire for genuine connection and his fear of being hurt again raged on, shaping the person he would become. This chapter delves into Asher's complexities, exploring the reasons behind his behavior and its impact on those around him. It sets the stage for his eventual reckoning and the possibility of redemption in the chapters to come.

CHAPTER 3
THE NEW GIRL

CHARLOTTE'S ARRIVAL

Introduction of Charlotte: A Transfer Student with a Bright Personality and Unique Charm

The buzz around school was palpable when the news of a new student spread. Charlotte Thompson, a transfer student from a different state, was set to join Asher's high school in the middle of the semester. The anticipation was high, with everyone curious about the newcomer. Charlotte made her grand entrance on a crisp autumn morning. She walked into the school with an air of confidence that immediately caught everyone's attention.

Charlotte was not just any new student; she had a unique charm that set her apart. She had shoulder-length auburn hair that shimmered in the sunlight, expressive hazel eyes that seemed to twinkle with mischief, and a radiant smile that could light up the darkest room. Her style was a mix of bohemian and classic, giving her a distinctive look that was both approachable and intriguing. Charlotte's personality was equally captivating. She was warm and friendly and had a natural ability to make people feel comfortable around her. Her laughter was infectious, and she carried herself with a grace and poise that belied her age.

Asher's Initial Intrigue and Curiosity about the New Girl

Asher first noticed Charlotte during lunch break. She was sitting alone at a table, unpacking her lunch with a serene expression on her face. There was something about her that immediately drew his attention. Maybe it was her relaxed demeanor amidst the chaos of the school cafeteria or the way she seemed completely at ease in her own company. Asher watched her from a distance, intrigued by her presence.

His curiosity grew as he observed her over the next few days. Charlotte quickly became a topic of conversation among the students. She was friendly and open, easily making friends and fitting into various social circles. Asher couldn't help but feel a spark of interest. Unlike the other girls he had dated, Charlotte seemed different – she was not trying to impress anyone, and there was a genuine quality about her that was hard to ignore.

FIRST INTERACTION

The First Meeting: Witty Banter and a Hint of Chemistry

Asher knew he had to meet Charlotte. His initial approach was casual; he didn't want to seem too eager. He waited for the right moment, which came one afternoon when he saw Charlotte struggling with her locker. Asher seized the opportunity and walked over with a confident smile. "Need some help?" he asked, his tone light and friendly.

Charlotte looked up, her hazel eyes meeting his. She smiled warmly. "Yes, actually. This locker seems to have a mind of its own," she replied, her voice carrying a hint of amusement. Asher stepped in, quickly fixing the jammed lock with a practiced ease. "There you go," he said, stepping back.

"Thanks, Asher, right?" Charlotte said, extending her hand. Asher was momentarily taken aback that she knew his name. "Yeah, and you're Charlotte," he replied, shaking her hand. The touch was brief but electric, a subtle hint of the chemistry between them.

Their conversation flowed naturally from there, filled with witty banter and laughter. Asher found himself genuinely enjoying their exchange, something he hadn't felt in a long time. Charlotte was quick-witted and sharp, matching him comment for comment. There was an ease to their interaction, a sense of familiarity despite just having met.

Asher's Determination to Win Her Over

After their first interaction, Asher's interest in Charlotte intensified. Initially, he saw her as just another conquest, a new challenge to his charm and charisma. However, something about Charlotte made him want to put in more effort. She was not like the other girls he had dated; she was neither easily impressed nor intimidated by his reputation.

Asher decided to approach this challenge with a blend of his usual tactics and a newfound sincerity. He began by learning more about Charlotte – her interests, hobbies, and the things that made her tick. He discovered she loved painting, much like he once did, and had a passion for photography. Asher used this information to his advantage, planning ways to incorporate these interests into his attempts to win her over.

He started by casually joining the art club, where Charlotte spent most of her free time. At first, he watched from a distance, admiring her skill and dedication. Then, he began to engage with her more directly, asking her about her work and sharing his own experiences with art. Their shared interest became a bridge, allowing them to connect on a deeper level.

Asher also planned a series of thoughtful gestures. He would leave small, hand-drawn sketches in her locker, reminiscent of his earlier attempts to catch Amanda's attention but with more genuine intent. He arranged for them to go on outings to art galleries and photography exhibits, knowing these were places where Charlotte felt most inspired.

Despite his initial intentions, Asher found himself genuinely enjoying the time he spent with Charlotte. She challenged him in ways no one else had, making him question his own motives and actions. For the first time in a long while, Asher felt a connection that went beyond the superficial, a connection that made him reconsider his approach to relationships and his fear of vulnerability.

Reflection

Charlotte's arrival marked a turning point in Asher's life. She was not just another girl he could charm and leave behind; she was someone who made him want to be better. Their first meeting was more than just an introduction; it was the beginning of a journey that would challenge Asher's views on love, trust, and vulnerability. The chemistry between them hinted at the possibility of something deeper, something that could potentially change Asher's life forever. This chapter sets the stage for the development of their relationship, highlighting the initial sparks and the challenges Asher faces as he navigates his feelings for Charlotte.

CHAPTER 4

THE FIRST DATE

PLANNING THE DATE

Asher's Preparation for Their First Date: Choosing an Impressive Location

Asher wanted the first date with Charlotte to be perfect. He knew he had to do something special to impress her, something that would reflect both of their interests and create a memorable experience. After much thought, he decided on a quaint, art-themed café located in the heart of the city. The café was known for its cozy atmosphere, adorned with local artists' work, and featured an outdoor garden where patrons could enjoy their coffee surrounded by nature.

To make the date even more special, Asher planned an itinerary that included a visit to a nearby art gallery that was hosting an exhibition of contemporary art. He knew Charlotte would appreciate the creativity and thoughtfulness behind his choice. Asher spent days preparing, making reservations, and even brushing up on some art history to impress Charlotte with his knowledge.

On the day of the date, Asher meticulously dressed in a casual yet stylish outfit – a crisp white shirt, dark jeans, and a leather jacket. He wanted to look his best without appearing too formal. He arrived early at the café to ensure everything was perfect, from the table placement to the flowers he had arranged to be on their table.

Charlotte's Mixed Feelings and Excitement about Going Out with Asher

Charlotte, on the other hand, had mixed feelings about the date. While she was undeniably excited, she couldn't help but feel a bit nervous. She had heard about Asher's reputation and was aware of his charm and past as a player. However, their interactions so far had shown her a different side of him – one that was thoughtful, genuine, and sincere.

As she got ready for the date, Charlotte chose a simple yet elegant dress that highlighted her artistic personality. She decided to wear a light blue sundress with a floral pattern, paired with a denim jacket and comfortable sandals. She styled her auburn hair in loose waves, allowing it to flow naturally. Her heart raced with anticipation and a hint of anxiety, wondering if this date would mark the beginning of something special or just be another fleeting encounter.

THE DATE

A Detailed Account of Their First Date

Asher picked up Charlotte right on time, greeting her with a warm smile and a bouquet of daisies, her favorite flowers. Charlotte was pleasantly surprised by the gesture, her initial nerves easing as they drove to the café. The ride was filled with light conversation and laughter, setting a comfortable tone for the evening.

When they arrived at the café, Charlotte was immediately charmed by the cozy, artistic ambiance. The walls were adorned with vibrant paintings, and the soft hum of background music added to the relaxed atmosphere. Asher had reserved a table in the garden area, where twinkling fairy lights created a magical setting.

They started with coffee and pastries, engaging in easy conversation. Asher and Charlotte discussed their favorite artists, shared stories from their childhood, and found common ground in their love for creativity. Asher listened intently as Charlotte talked about her passion for photography, admiring the way her eyes lit up when she spoke. In turn, he shared his own experiences with drawing and how it had been a refuge for him during his younger years.

After their coffee, they made their way to the art gallery. The exhibition was a perfect choice, featuring a mix of abstract and contemporary pieces that sparked deep conversations between them. Asher and Charlotte walked through the gallery, discussing their interpretations of the artworks and the emotions they evoked. Asher was impressed by Charlotte's insights and found himself genuinely enjoying her company.

One particular painting caught their attention – a large, colorful abstract piece that seemed to capture the chaos and beauty of life. They stood in front of it for a while, sharing their thoughts and feelings. It was in this moment that Asher realized he was seeing Charlotte in a new light. She was not just another girl he was trying to impress; she was someone who inspired him and made him want to be better.

The Beginning of a Genuine Connection

As the evening progressed, Asher and Charlotte's connection deepened. They ended the date with a walk through a nearby park, the night air cool and refreshing. They talked about their dreams and aspirations, their fears, and the experiences that had shaped them. Asher felt a sense of ease and openness with Charlotte that he hadn't felt with anyone in a long time.

At the end of the night, Asher walked Charlotte to her door. There was a moment of hesitation before he leaned in and gently kissed her cheek. "Thank you for a wonderful evening, Charlotte," he said softly. She smiled, her heart fluttering. "Thank you, Asher. I had a great time," she replied.

As Asher walked away, he couldn't help but feel a sense of hope and excitement. For the first time in years, he felt a genuine connection with someone, and it both thrilled and terrified him. Charlotte, too, felt a mix of emotions – a spark of something new and the cautious optimism that comes with the beginning of a potential relationship.

Reflection

This chapter marked the beginning of a transformative journey for Asher. The date with Charlotte was more than just a night out; it was a turning point that challenged his views on love and vulnerability. The genuine connection they shared was a stark contrast to his previous superficial relationships, and it set the stage for the changes that would unfold in his life. Asher's first date with Charlotte was a beautiful blend of art, conversation, and the blossoming of something real and meaningful.

CHAPTER 5
A CHANGE OF HEART

GROWING FEELINGS

Asher's Growing Affection for Charlotte and His Confusion Over These Unfamiliar Emotions

As the weeks passed, Asher found himself thinking about Charlotte more and more. Their first date had been a revelation, and every subsequent interaction only deepened his feelings for her. Unlike his previous conquests, Charlotte was not just a fleeting interest. She was someone who made him feel alive in ways he had never experienced before.

Asher's growing affection for Charlotte brought a wave of unfamiliar emotions. He felt a warmth in his chest whenever he saw her, a genuine happiness that was new to him. He looked forward to their conversations, whether in person or through text, and found himself smiling at the smallest things she did. This was more than a physical attraction; it was an emotional connection that scared and thrilled him at the same time.

He often found himself lost in thought, replaying moments they had shared and imagining a future with her. This confusion over his feelings led to sleepless nights, where he would lie awake, grappling with the depth of his emotions. For the first time, Asher was falling in love, and it was both exhilarating and terrifying.

Moments That Show Asher's Softer Side, His Vulnerability Around Charlotte

Charlotte had a way of bringing out Asher's softer side. Around her, he felt safe enough to let his guard down and show his vulnerability. One evening, as they sat on a bench in the park, watching the sunset, Asher opened up about his past. He told Charlotte about his childhood, his love for drawing, and the heartbreak that had changed him.

Charlotte listened intently, her hand gently squeezing his in reassurance. "It's okay to be vulnerable, Asher," she said softly. "It's part of being human."

Asher felt a lump in his throat, her words resonating deeply within him. At that moment, he realized how much he trusted her and how much he wanted to be the person she believed he could be. He shared his fears and insecurities, things he had never told anyone before. And Charlotte, with her kind eyes and understanding smile, accepted him for who he was.

Another moment of vulnerability came when Charlotte fell ill. Asher took it upon himself to take care of her, bringing her soup, medicine, and a stack of her favorite movies. He stayed by her side, comforting her and making sure she felt loved and cared for. It was a simple act, but it showed the depth of his feelings and his willingness to be there for her, no matter what.

INTERNAL STRUGGLE

Asher's Battle with His Past Behavior and the Fear of Hurting Charlotte

Despite his growing feelings for Charlotte, Asher was haunted by his past. He had hurt many girls, leaving a trail of broken hearts in his wake. The fear of repeating those mistakes with Charlotte gnawed at him constantly. He didn't want to hurt her, but he wasn't sure if he was capable of maintaining a healthy, loving relationship.

Asher's internal struggle was intense. He would often find himself withdrawing, fearing that his old habits would resurface. He was scared of letting Charlotte down, of being the cause of her pain. This fear sometimes manifested in self-sabotaging behavior, where he would create distance between them, hoping to protect her from himself.

There were moments when Asher felt overwhelmed by guilt. He would see the hurt expressions of the girls he had dated in his mind, their faces a constant reminder of his past mistakes. He didn't want Charlotte to become another victim of his inability to commit. This battle with his conscience was a daily struggle, one that left him feeling emotionally exhausted and conflicted.

His Attempts to Change, Driven by His Desire to Be Worthy of Charlotte's Love

Despite his fears, Asher was determined to change. He wanted to be worthy of Charlotte's love, to become the kind of person who could make her happy. This desire drove him to make significant changes in his life. He started by seeking advice from trusted friends and mentors, opening up about his struggles and asking for guidance.

Asher also began to reflect on his actions, recognizing patterns of behavior that needed to be addressed. He made a conscious effort to be more honest and transparent with Charlotte, sharing his thoughts and feelings openly. He worked on building trust, proving through his actions that he was committed to their relationship.

One of the most significant steps Asher took was to reconnect with his artistic side. Drawing had always been a part of him, a way to express his emotions. He started sketching again, creating pieces that reflected his journey of self-discovery and growth. He even shared some of his drawings with Charlotte, who was delighted to see this side of him.

Asher also became more involved in activities that brought him closer to Charlotte's world. He joined her in photography outings, attended art classes together, and supported her in her pursuits. These experiences not only strengthened their bond but also helped Asher see the beauty in being vulnerable and open to love.

In moments of doubt, Asher would remind himself of the reasons he wanted to change. He thought about

Charlotte's smile, her laughter, and the way she made him feel. These thoughts gave him the strength to continue his journey of transformation, despite the challenges and setbacks he faced.

Reflection

Chapter 5 marks a pivotal point in Asher's story, as he grapples with his growing feelings for Charlotte and the internal struggle that accompanies them. His journey towards change is driven by a genuine desire to be a better person, worthy of Charlotte's love. This chapter highlights the complexities of love, vulnerability, and personal growth, setting the stage for Asher's continued development and the deepening of his relationship with Charlotte.

CHAPTER 6
THE CONFESSION

THE DECISION TO CONFESS

Asher's Realization That He Needs to Be Honest with Charlotte About His Past

Asher's relationship with Charlotte continued to deepen, and with each passing day, his feelings for her grew stronger. However, his past weighed heavily on his conscience. He knew that if he wanted to build a future with Charlotte, he had to come clean about his previous behavior. The guilt and fear of losing her were overwhelming, but he understood that honesty was the foundation of any strong relationship.

The decision to confess was not an easy one. It came to him one evening as he watched Charlotte laugh at a joke he made. Her laughter was genuine, her eyes sparkling with joy, and in that moment, Asher felt a pang of guilt so sharp it almost took his breath away. He realized that he could no longer keep his past hidden; it wasn't fair to Charlotte, and it wasn't fair to their relationship. Asher knew he had to tell her the truth, no matter the consequences.

The Anxiety and Fear Leading Up to His Confession

In the days leading up to the confession, Asher was a bundle of nerves. He struggled with the fear of losing Charlotte, the anxiety of how she would react, and the dread of seeing her hurt because of him. His thoughts were consumed by the impending conversation, making it difficult to focus on anything else.

Asher rehearsed what he would say over and over again, each time feeling more anxious than before. He knew there was no perfect way to reveal his past, but he hoped that his honesty would show Charlotte how much he had changed and how deeply he cared for her. Despite his fears, Asher was determined to go through with it. He could no longer bear the weight of his secrets.

CHARLOTTE'S REACTION

The Moment Asher Confesses His Past Actions to Charlotte

The day of the confession finally arrived. Asher invited Charlotte to his apartment, choosing a quiet, private setting where they could talk without interruptions. They sat on the couch, and Asher took a deep breath, gathering his thoughts and courage.

"Charlotte, there's something I need to tell you," he began, his voice trembling slightly. Charlotte looked at him with concern, sensing the seriousness of the moment. Asher took her hand in his, his eyes filled with sincerity and regret. "I haven't been completely honest with you about my past. Before I met you, I wasn't a good person when it came to relationships. I hurt a lot of people, played with their feelings, and treated them badly. I was scared of being vulnerable, so I pushed people away before they could hurt me."

Asher paused, searching Charlotte's face for a reaction. Her expression was a mix of confusion and worry, but she remained silent, allowing him to continue. "Meeting you changed everything for me," Asher continued, his voice breaking with emotion. "I fell for you in a way I never thought was possible, and I realized that I needed to be better, to be worthy of your love. But I can't build our relationship on lies. You deserve to know the truth."

Charlotte's Initial Shock, Hurt, and Decision to Take a Break from Their Relationship

Charlotte listened to Asher's confession, her initial shock turning into hurt and disbelief. The weight of his words sank in, and she pulled her hand away from his, standing up to put some distance between them. "Asher, I don't know what to say," she finally replied, her voice trembling. "I appreciate your honesty, but this is a lot to take in. You've hurt so many people, and I can't just ignore that."

Tears welled up in her eyes as she struggled to process everything. "I need some time to think," Charlotte said, her voice barely above a whisper. "I need to figure out if I can trust you after this." Asher's heart shattered at her words, the fear of losing her becoming a harsh reality. "I understand," he said quietly, his own eyes brimming with tears. "Take all the time you need. I'm so sorry for everything, Charlotte. I just want you to know that I love you, and I'll do whatever it takes to make things right."

Charlotte nodded, unable to say anything more. She gathered her things and left Asher's apartment, leaving him alone with his thoughts and regrets.

Asher's Heartbreak and Regret Over His Past

Asher stood in the middle of his apartment, feeling the weight of his actions crashing down on him. He had hoped that honesty would bring them closer, but instead, it had pushed Charlotte away. The silence of the room was deafening, and he felt an overwhelming sense of despair and loneliness.

In the days that followed, Asher was consumed by regret. He replayed the confession in his mind, wishing he could take back the pain he had caused Charlotte. He realized how deeply his past actions had hurt not just the girls he had dated, but now the one person he truly loved. The guilt was unbearable, and Asher found himself questioning if he would ever be able to make amends.

He tried to reach out to Charlotte, sending her messages of apology and reassurance, but she remained distant, needing time and space to process everything. Asher's heart ached with every passing day, the fear of losing her becoming more real. He knew that he had to respect her need for distance, but it didn't make the waiting any easier.

Reflection

Chapter 6 captures the raw and emotional moment of Asher's confession and its immediate aftermath. His decision to be honest with Charlotte about his past is a significant step in his journey toward redemption, but it also brings to light the consequences of his previous actions. Charlotte's initial shock and hurt, and her decision to take a break from their relationship, highlight the impact of Asher's past on their present and future. This chapter sets the stage for the challenges they will face as they navigate their feelings and decide whether their love is strong enough to overcome the shadows of Asher's past.

CHAPTER 7
THE REUNION

TIME APART

Charlotte's Process of Reflection, Talking to Friends, and Understanding Her Feelings

After leaving Asher's apartment, Charlotte was overwhelmed with emotions. The weight of Asher's confession was heavy, and she needed time to process it. She retreated to her apartment, seeking solitude and clarity. The first few days were the hardest; her mind was a whirlwind of thoughts and feelings. She felt betrayed, hurt, and confused, but there was also a part of her that still loved Asher and wanted to believe in his ability to change.

Charlotte decided to confide in her close friends, hoping they could provide some perspective. She invited her best friends, Sarah and Emily, over for a heart-to-heart discussion. Over cups of tea and comforting words, Charlotte poured out her heart, explaining everything Asher had told her. Sarah and Emily listened intently, offering their support and advice.

"People can change, Charlotte," Sarah said thoughtfully. "But it takes time and effort. You need to figure out if you're willing to give him that chance."

Emily nodded in agreement. "Trust is hard to rebuild, but it's not impossible. If you still have feelings for him, maybe it's worth seeing if he can prove himself."

Their words gave Charlotte a lot to think about. She spent the next few weeks reflecting on her feelings and weighing the pros and cons. She revisited the moments she had shared with Asher, remembering his kindness, his vulnerability, and the genuine connection they had. She also considered the pain his past actions had caused and the risk of being hurt again. Gradually, Charlotte began to understand that her feelings for Asher were strong, and she owed it to herself to see if their relationship could withstand the test of time.

Asher's Attempts to Show He Has Truly Changed: Small Acts of Kindness and Sincerity

During their time apart, Asher was determined to prove to Charlotte that he had genuinely changed. He knew words alone wouldn't be enough; he had to demonstrate his transformation through actions. He started with small, thoughtful gestures that showed his sincerity and commitment.

Asher began by sending Charlotte handwritten letters, expressing his feelings and apologizing for his past behavior. In these letters, he shared his journey of self-discovery, his regrets, and his hopes for their future. Each letter was a heartfelt testament to his love for her and his desire to make things right.

In addition to the letters, Asher made a conscious effort to improve himself. He sought out therapy to address his past issues and to learn how to build healthier relationships. He also reconnected with his artistic side, pouring his emotions into his drawings and sharing some of his artwork with Charlotte. He hoped that these actions would show her that he was committed to becoming a better person.

Asher also reached out to some of the girls he had hurt in the past, offering sincere apologies and seeking forgiveness. It was a difficult and humbling experience, but it was a necessary step in his journey of redemption. He wanted to make amends not just for Charlotte, but for himself as well.

FORGIVENESS

The Heartfelt Conversation Where Charlotte Forgives Asher

After weeks of reflection and soul-searching, Charlotte felt ready to talk to Asher. She invited him to meet her at the park where they had spent so many happy moments together. Asher arrived early, his heart pounding with anticipation and hope. He saw Charlotte approaching and stood up, his eyes filled with a mixture of anxiety and longing.

They sat down on a bench, and for a moment, there was only silence. Finally, Charlotte took a deep breath and began to speak. "Asher, these past few weeks have been really hard. I've been trying to sort through my feelings and understand what I want. Your letters meant a lot to me, and I can see that you're trying to change."

Asher nodded, his throat tight with emotion. "I love you, Charlotte. I know I've made mistakes, but I'm doing everything I can to be better. I want to earn your trust and be the person you deserve."

Charlotte looked into his eyes, seeing the sincerity and regret there. "I still love you too, Asher. But trust is something that needs to be rebuilt. I need to know that you're committed to this, to us."

"I am," Asher replied earnestly. "I'll do whatever it takes to prove it to you. I've started therapy, I've been making amends, and I'm working on myself every day. I want to be worthy of your love."

Tears filled Charlotte's eyes as she reached out and took his hand. "I believe you, Asher. And I'm willing to give us another chance. But we need to take it one step at a time, together."

Asher squeezed her hand, his heart swelling with relief and gratitude. "Thank you, Charlotte. I promise you won't regret it."

Their Emotional Reunion and Renewed Commitment to Each Other

The conversation marked the beginning of their reunion, but it was only the first step in a long journey. Asher and Charlotte spent the next few weeks rebuilding their relationship, taking things slowly and focusing on open communication and mutual support. They went on dates, revisited their favorite spots, and created new memories together.

Asher continued to show his commitment through small acts of kindness, like surprising Charlotte with her favorite flowers, cooking her dinner, or simply being there to listen when she needed to talk. Charlotte, in turn, opened her heart to him, allowing herself to trust and believe in their future.

Their renewed commitment to each other was evident in every interaction. They were more honest, more vulnerable, and more supportive than ever before. Asher and Charlotte had both grown and changed, and their relationship was stronger for it.

One evening, as they walked hand-in-hand through the park, Charlotte stopped and turned to Asher. "I'm proud of you," she said softly. "You've come so far, and I'm grateful to have you in my life."

Asher smiled, pulling her into a gentle embrace. "I couldn't have done it without you, Charlotte. You're my inspiration, my everything."

They stood there, wrapped in each other's arms, knowing that their love had survived its greatest test. It was a love that had been forged in the fire of honesty, growth, and forgiveness, and it was stronger than ever. Asher and Charlotte were ready to face the future together, with a renewed sense of hope and commitment.

Reflection

Chapter 7 highlights the power of love, forgiveness, and personal growth. Charlotte's process of reflection and Asher's sincere efforts to change pave the way for their emotional reunion. Their heartfelt conversation and renewed commitment to each other mark a turning point in their relationship, showing that true love can overcome even the deepest of challenges. This chapter sets the stage for the continued development of their bond and the bright future they are building together.

CHAPTER 8

BUILDING TRUST

EFFORTS TO REBUILD TRUST

The Challenges They Face in Rebuilding Trust, Dealing with Insecurities and Past Wounds

Rebuilding trust was not an easy journey for Asher and Charlotte. Their renewed commitment to each other marked the beginning of a challenging process filled with ups and downs. Both had to confront their insecurities and address the past wounds that still lingered.

Charlotte struggled with feelings of doubt and fear. Despite her decision to give Asher another chance, there were moments when she questioned if she had made the right choice. Memories of Asher's confession and the hurt it had caused would sometimes resurface, making it difficult for her to fully trust him. She feared that history might repeat itself and that she would end up heartbroken once again.

Asher, on the other hand, grappled with guilt and anxiety. He was determined to prove himself to Charlotte, but he was also afraid of making mistakes. Every interaction was a test of his sincerity and commitment. He knew that any slip-up could shatter the fragile trust they were working to rebuild. Asher was constantly on edge, trying to balance his desire to be open and vulnerable with the need to show strength and reliability.

Instances of Asher Proving His Loyalty and Devotion

Despite the challenges, Asher made continuous efforts to prove his loyalty and devotion to Charlotte. He understood that actions spoke louder than words, and he was committed to showing her that he had truly changed.

One instance that stood out was when Asher was approached by an old acquaintance who tried to rekindle their previous fling. Asher immediately shut down the conversation, making it clear that he was in a committed relationship with Charlotte. He later told

Charlotte about the encounter, emphasizing his dedication to their relationship. This honesty and transparency helped to build her confidence in him.

Asher also went out of his way to support Charlotte in her pursuits. When she had a photography exhibition, he was there every step of the way, helping her set up, offering encouragement, and proudly showcasing her work to everyone he knew. His genuine pride in her accomplishments and his unwavering support were clear signs of his commitment.

There were also small, everyday acts that demonstrated Asher's loyalty. He made it a point to keep Charlotte informed about his whereabouts, never wanting her to worry or feel uncertain. He would send her messages throughout the day, just to let her know he was thinking of her. These consistent efforts, though seemingly minor, played a crucial role in rebuilding trust.

Charlotte's Gradual Process of Fully Trusting Asher Again

For Charlotte, learning to fully trust Asher again was a gradual process. She knew it wouldn't happen overnight and that it required both patience and effort. She focused on the positive changes she saw in Asher and the sincerity in his actions.

Charlotte began by acknowledging her own feelings and communicating openly with Asher about her fears and doubts. They had long, heartfelt conversations where she expressed her concerns and Asher listened attentively, offering reassurance and understanding. These conversations were cathartic and helped to clear the air, allowing them to move forward with greater clarity.

Over time, Charlotte started to notice a shift in her perception. She saw how Asher consistently prioritized their relationship, how he was always there for her, and how he made a genuine effort to be a better person. These observations gradually eased her doubts and built a foundation of trust.

There were moments when Charlotte tested the waters, giving Asher opportunities to prove himself. Whether it was relying on him during stressful times or trusting him with personal matters, Asher never faltered. Each successful instance strengthened her belief in him and in their relationship.

STRENGTHENING RELATIONSHIP

The Ways They Strengthen Their Bond, Through Shared Activities, Open Communication, and Mutual Support

Asher and Charlotte realized that rebuilding trust was intertwined with strengthening their bond. They focused on shared activities, open communication, and mutual support to reinforce their connection and create new, positive memories.

Shared Activities

They engaged in activities that they both enjoyed, such as art and photography. Asher would accompany Charlotte on her photography outings, helping her find interesting subjects and locations. They also spent time painting together, a hobby that allowed them to express their creativity and emotions. These shared experiences brought them closer and provided a sense of unity.

They also explored new hobbies together. They took cooking classes, went hiking, and even tried their hand at ballroom dancing. These activities not only strengthened their bond but also created a sense of adventure and excitement in their relationship.

Open Communication

Open communication became the cornerstone of their relationship. They made it a point to have regular check-ins, discussing their feelings, concerns, and aspirations. These conversations were candid and heartfelt, fostering a deeper understanding of each other.

Asher and Charlotte also set aside time for weekly "date nights," where they would go out for dinner or have a cozy night in. During these dates, they would focus on each other, putting away their phones and distractions. These moments of undivided attention were crucial in maintaining their connection and ensuring that they stayed in tune with each other's needs.

Mutual Support

Mutual support played a significant role in strengthening their relationship. Asher was Charlotte's biggest cheerleader, always encouraging her to pursue her dreams and standing by her side during challenging times. Likewise, Charlotte supported Asher in his journey of self-improvement, attending therapy sessions with him and celebrating his milestones.

They learned to lean on each other, providing emotional and practical support. When Charlotte faced a difficult project at work, Asher helped her brainstorm ideas and offered a listening ear. When Asher struggled with his own insecurities, Charlotte was there to reassure him and remind him of his worth.

Their mutual support extended to their families and friends as well. They made an effort to integrate their lives, attending family gatherings, and social events together. This integration created a sense of belonging and reinforced their commitment to each other.

Reflection

Chapter 8 captures the intricate process of rebuilding trust and strengthening the bond between Asher and Charlotte. Their journey is marked by challenges, but their dedication to each other and their relationship shines through. Through shared activities, open communication, and mutual support, they create a strong foundation built on love, trust, and respect. This chapter highlights the importance of perseverance, patience, and the power of genuine connection in overcoming obstacles and building a lasting, meaningful relationship.

CHAPTER 9
THE PROPOSAL

ASHER'S PLANS

Asher's Elaborate Plan to Propose: Seeking the Perfect Moment and Place

Asher had been contemplating the perfect way to propose to Charlotte for months. He wanted the proposal to be a reflection of their journey together and a promise of the beautiful future he envisioned for them. After much thought, he decided that the ideal place would be the art-themed café where they had their first date. It was a place filled with happy memories and represented the beginning of their love story.

Asher's plan was elaborate and meticulously crafted. He wanted every detail to be perfect, from the setting to the timing. He decided to propose during the café's annual art exhibition, which would provide the perfect backdrop for his artistic and romantic proposal. Asher contacted the café's owner and arranged for a private area to be set up with twinkling fairy lights, candles, and some of his and Charlotte's favorite artworks displayed around the space.

Asher also chose a date that held special significance for them – the anniversary of their first date. He wanted the proposal to be a celebration of their journey and the love they had built together. He spent weeks planning every detail, ensuring that everything would be perfect for Charlotte.

Involvement of Friends and Family to Make the Proposal Special

Asher knew that involving their friends and family would make the proposal even more special for Charlotte. He reached out to her best friends, Sarah and Emily, and shared his plan with them. They were thrilled and immediately offered their help, eager to make the moment unforgettable.

Asher also spoke with Charlotte's parents, seeking their blessing and support. They were touched by his sincerity and happily agreed to be a part of the proposal. Asher's parents were equally supportive and excited, offering their assistance in any way they could.

Together, they devised a plan to surprise Charlotte. On the day of the proposal, Sarah and Emily would take her out for a girls' day, keeping her occupied while Asher and the rest of their friends and family prepared the café. Charlotte's parents would be present at the café, hidden from view until the big moment.

Asher also enlisted the help of a local photographer to capture the special moment. He wanted to ensure that they would have beautiful photographs to remember the day by. With everything in place, Asher felt a mix of excitement and nervousness as the day approached.

THE PROPOSAL MOMENT

The Romantic and Heartfelt Proposal: Capturing Charlotte's Surprise and Joy

The day of the proposal arrived, and everything was set. Asher could hardly contain his excitement as he waited for the evening. Sarah and Emily had taken Charlotte out for brunch and a spa day, ensuring that she would be relaxed and happy. As the sun began to set, they told Charlotte that they had one more surprise for her and drove her to the café.

When Charlotte arrived, she was puzzled to see the café closed to the public. Sarah and Emily led her to the private area that Asher had prepared. As they walked in, Charlotte gasped in surprise. The twinkling fairy lights, the candles, and the beautiful artworks created a magical atmosphere. She looked around, her eyes wide with wonder, and then she saw Asher standing at the center of the room, a bouquet of daisies in his hand.

Asher's heart pounded as he walked towards Charlotte, taking her hands in his. "Charlotte, from the moment I met you, you've brought so much joy and love into my life," he began, his voice filled with emotion. "You've stood by me through the good times and the bad, and you've shown me what it means to truly love and be loved. I can't imagine my life without you, and I don't want to. I want to spend the rest of my life making you as happy as you've made me."

Asher knelt down on one knee, holding out a beautiful engagement ring. "Charlotte Thompson, will you marry me?"

Tears filled Charlotte's eyes as she looked at Asher, her heart swelling with joy and love. "Yes, Asher," she said, her voice choked with emotion. "Yes, I'll marry you!"

Asher slipped the ring onto her finger and stood up, pulling her into a tight embrace. Their friends and family, who had been watching from a distance, erupted into cheers and applause. Charlotte looked around, realizing that everyone she loved was there to share in their special moment.

Their Engagement and the Excitement of Planning Their Future Together

The rest of the evening was filled with celebration and joy. Asher and Charlotte's friends and family joined them, congratulating the newly engaged couple and sharing in their happiness. The café was filled with laughter, music, and the warmth of love and support.

Asher and Charlotte spent the night talking about their future, dreaming about their wedding and the life they would build together. They discussed their hopes and aspirations, excitedly planning the details of their special day. They knew that there would be challenges ahead, but they were confident in their love and their ability to overcome anything together.

In the days and weeks that followed, Asher and Charlotte began planning their wedding in earnest. They visited venues, chose their bridal party, and picked out their wedding attire. Every decision was made with care and consideration, reflecting their unique personalities and the love they shared.

Their engagement period was a time of excitement and anticipation, but it was also a time of deepening their bond. As they navigated the planning process, they continued to support each other, communicating openly and working together as a team. Their love grew stronger with each passing day, and they looked forward to the future with hope and joy.

Reflection

Chapter 9 captures the beauty and emotion of Asher's proposal to Charlotte. His elaborate plan, the involvement of friends and family, and the heartfelt proposal moment all contribute to a memorable and touching experience. Their engagement marks the beginning of a new chapter in their lives, filled with excitement and the promise of a shared future. This chapter highlights the importance of love, commitment, and the support of loved ones in building a lasting and meaningful relationship.

CHAPTER 10
HAPPILY EVER AFTER

THE WEDDING

The Beautiful and Emotional Wedding Ceremony, Surrounded by Loved Ones

The day of Asher and Charlotte's wedding was one of pure magic and emotion. The ceremony took place at a picturesque vineyard, surrounded by rolling hills and vibrant grapevines. The sun shone brightly, casting a warm, golden glow over the entire setting. Friends and family gathered, their hearts filled with joy and anticipation.

Charlotte looked stunning in her elegant, lace-trimmed gown, her auburn hair cascading in soft waves. Asher, dressed in a tailored navy suit, stood at the altar, his eyes fixed on Charlotte as she walked down the aisle. His heart swelled with love and gratitude, knowing that he was about to marry the woman who had transformed his life.

The ceremony was intimate and heartfelt. Asher and Charlotte chose to write their own vows, each word reflecting their journey and the deep bond they shared. Charlotte's voice trembled with emotion as she spoke:

"Asher, from the moment we met, you have brought light and love into my life. You have shown me the beauty of vulnerability and the strength of commitment. I promise to stand by you, to support you, and to love you with all my heart, for all the days of our lives."

Asher took her hands in his, his voice steady but filled with emotion:

"Charlotte, you have taught me what it means to truly love and be loved. You have been my rock, my inspiration, and my greatest joy. I promise to cherish you, to honor you, and to be the best partner I can be. Together, we will face the future with hope and love, always."

As they exchanged rings, their eyes locked, and the world seemed to fade away. The moment they were pronounced husband and wife, the vineyard erupted in applause and cheers. Asher and Charlotte shared their first kiss as a married couple, a kiss filled with the promise of a lifetime of love and happiness.

The reception was a lively celebration of their love, with heartfelt toasts, dancing under the stars, and a sense of joy that permeated the entire evening. Asher and Charlotte's families and friends shared in their happiness, creating memories that would last a lifetime.

LIFE TOGETHER

A Glimpse into Their Happy Life Together, with Three Children (Clara, Max, Ash) and a Loving Family Dynamic

Asher and Charlotte's life together was filled with love, laughter, and the joys of raising a family. They settled into a cozy home in a friendly neighborhood, where they welcomed their three beautiful children: Clara, Max, and Ash. Each child brought their own unique energy and personality to the family, enriching their lives in countless ways.

Clara, the eldest, was a creative soul with a passion for painting, much like her father. She spent hours in her room, creating vibrant artworks that adorned the walls of their home. Max, the older twin, was adventurous and full of energy, always exploring and discovering new things. Ash, the younger twin, was a gentle and thoughtful child, with a love for nature and animals.

Asher and Charlotte embraced the challenges and joys of parenthood together. They created a loving and supportive environment for their children, encouraging them to pursue their passions and to always be kind and compassionate. Their home was filled with laughter, whether it was during family game nights, impromptu dance parties in the living room, or quiet moments of reading bedtime stories.

Moments of Joy, Challenges, and the Enduring Love That Binds Them

Life was not without its challenges, but Asher and Charlotte faced them together, their love and commitment serving as a guiding light. They navigated the ups and downs of parenthood, career changes, and the everyday stresses of life, always finding strength in each other.

There were moments of pure joy, like watching Clara win her first art competition, seeing Max conquer his fear of swimming, and witnessing Ash's gentle care for a stray kitten they found. These moments filled their hearts with pride and happiness, reinforcing the deep love they had for their children and each other.

There were also times of struggle, like when Asher faced a setback in his career or when Charlotte dealt with a health scare. During these difficult times, they leaned on each other, providing comfort and support. They communicated openly, worked through their problems together, and emerged stronger each time.

Their enduring love was evident in the small, everyday gestures – a loving glance across the room, a surprise date night, or simply holding hands during a walk in the park. Asher and Charlotte's relationship was a testament to the power of love, resilience, and mutual respect.

The Story Concludes with a Reflection on How Far Asher Has Come and the Happiness He Found with Charlotte

As the years passed, Asher often reflected on how far he had come. He remembered the shy, heartbroken boy he once was and the journey of transformation he had undergone. Meeting Charlotte had been the turning point in his life, and her love had given him the strength to change and grow into the man he was today.

Looking at his family, Asher felt a profound sense of gratitude and fulfillment. He had found a love that was true and enduring, a love that had brought him immense happiness and purpose. His journey had not been easy, but it had been worth every step.

Charlotte, too, felt a deep sense of contentment and joy. She had watched Asher grow and evolve, and she had shared in the beautiful moments and the challenges that had shaped their life together. Her love for him had only deepened over the years, and she cherished the family they had built.

Asher and Charlotte's story was one of love, redemption, and the power of commitment. Their journey had shown them that true happiness was found not in perfection, but in the willingness to grow, to forgive, and to love unconditionally. As they looked towards the future, they knew that whatever challenges lay ahead, they would face them together, their hearts forever intertwined.

The story of Asher and Charlotte concludes with a sense of hope and fulfillment. Their love had stood the test of time, and they had created a life filled with joy, love, and meaning. They had found their happily ever after, not in a fairy tale ending, but in the beautiful, messy, and wonderful reality of life together.

PART TWO
CLARA'S JOURNEY

INTRODUCTION

BRIEF RECAP OF CHARLOTTE AND ASHER'S LOVE STORY AND THEIR LIFE TOGETHER

A Summary of How Charlotte and Asher Met, Their Struggles and Triumphs, Their Marriage, and the Birth of Their Three Children

Charlotte and Asher's love story began in high school, a classic tale of boy meets girl, but with its own unique twists and turns. They met during their junior year, a serendipitous encounter that sparked an immediate connection. Charlotte, with her bright personality and unique charm, drew Asher in from the moment he saw her. Asher, who had a history of playing the field, found something different in

Charlotte – a sense of genuine connection and warmth that he had never experienced before.

Their relationship faced many challenges. Asher had to confront his past and prove that he had truly changed. Charlotte, on the other hand, had to learn to trust Asher despite his reputation. Their journey was not without its setbacks, but their love for each other and their commitment to growth and honesty helped them overcome these obstacles. They supported each other through college, started their careers, and eventually decided to get married.

Their wedding was a beautiful, emotional ceremony surrounded by loved ones. It marked the beginning of their shared life, filled with dreams and aspirations. Shortly after, they welcomed their first child, Clara, followed by twins, Max and Ash. The birth of their children brought immense joy and strengthened their bond. Together, they built a home filled with love, laughter, and mutual respect, providing a strong foundation for their family.

The Happiness and Love That Filled Their Home, Setting a Strong Foundation for Their Children

Charlotte and Asher's home was a haven of warmth and affection. They prioritized spending quality time together as a family, whether it was through shared meals, game nights, or outdoor adventures. Charlotte and Asher instilled values of kindness, empathy, and perseverance in their children, ensuring that they grew up in a nurturing environment. The love they shared for each other and their children was evident in every interaction, creating a strong sense of security and belonging for Clara, Max, and Ash.

INTRODUCTION OF THEIR THREE CHILDREN: CLARA, MAX, AND ASH

Description of Clara as the Eldest, Artistic and Introspective

Clara, the eldest of the three children, inherited her father's artistic talent and her mother's introspective nature. From a young age, she was drawn to creative pursuits, spending hours drawing, painting, and writing. Clara was a thoughtful and sensitive child, often lost in her own world of imagination. She had a quiet confidence about her, a gentle presence that brought calm to those around her. Clara's introspective nature made her wise beyond her years, and she often found solace in expressing her emotions through her art.

Max and Ash as the Younger Twins, Charismatic and Outgoing

Max and Ash, the younger twins, were a whirlwind of energy and charisma. They were inseparable, always up to some adventure or mischief. Max, the more outspoken of the two, had a natural charm that drew people to him. He was a star athlete, excelling in sports and always leading his team to victory. Ash, while equally charming, had a quieter confidence. He was known for his quick wit and intelligence, often surprising people with his insightful observations. Together, they formed a dynamic duo, always the life of the party and well-liked by their peers.

The Strong Family Bond They Share and the Individual Personalities of Each Child

Despite their differences, Clara, Max, and Ash shared a strong bond. They looked out for each other, supported each other through thick and thin, and had a deep sense of loyalty to their family. Clara was the nurturing older sister, always ready to offer a listening ear or a comforting hug. Max and Ash, while sometimes protective of Clara, often found themselves relying on her wisdom and calm demeanor.

Their individual personalities added richness to the family dynamic. Clara's artistic talents brought beauty and creativity into their lives. Max's athletic prowess and outgoing nature inspired confidence and teamwork. Ash's intelligence and humor added depth and joy to their interactions. Together, they created a harmonious blend of strengths and qualities that made their family unique.

SETTING THE STAGE FOR THE NEW STORY FOCUSED ON CLARA'S JOURNEY

Transition from the Parents' Love Story to the Challenges and Growth of Their Children, Particularly Clara

As Charlotte and Asher's story reached a point of stability and fulfillment, the focus shifted to the next generation. Clara, now a teenager, faced her own set of challenges and growth opportunities. Her journey would be marked by struggles to find her identity, navigate social dynamics, and cope with the pressures of high school. The strong foundation laid by her parents would play a crucial role in her ability to overcome these challenges and discover her true self.

Introduction of the Central Theme: Clara's Journey of Self-Discovery and Resilience

The central theme of this new story is Clara's journey of self-discovery and resilience. As she navigates the complexities of adolescence and the trials of high school, Clara will learn valuable lessons about herself and the world around her. Her experiences will test her strength, her relationships, and her sense of self-worth. Through it all, Clara will find her path, drawing on the love and support of her family and discovering her inner resilience. This journey will not only shape her as an individual but also highlight the enduring power of love, forgiveness, and personal growth.

CHAPTER 1

THE FIRST DAY OF HIGH SCHOOL

THE EXCITEMENT AND NERVOUSNESS OF CLARA, MAX, AND ASH ON THEIR FIRST DAY OF HIGH SCHOOL

Clara's Mixed Emotions as She Navigates the Excitement of a New Beginning and the Anxiety of Fitting In

Clara woke up early on the first day of high school, her heart a mix of excitement and trepidation. The crisp morning air was filled with anticipation as she carefully selected her outfit, wanting to make a good impression but also stay true to herself. She chose a simple, yet elegant ensemble: a flowy blouse, paired with her favorite jeans, and a pair of comfortable flats.

She stood in front of the mirror, taking a deep breath and giving herself a pep talk. Today was a new beginning, a chance to start fresh and find her place in the vast landscape of high school.

As she descended the stairs, she saw her brothers, Max and Ash, already buzzing with energy. They were animatedly discussing their plans for the day, their confidence radiating from every pore. Clara couldn't help but feel a twinge of envy at their ease and self-assuredness. She wanted to feel that way too, but the anxiety of fitting in and making friends gnawed at her.

Max and Ash's Confidence and Eagerness to Explore New Opportunities

Max and Ash were the epitome of teenage confidence. Their athletic builds and charismatic personalities made them naturals in social settings. They had spent the summer working out, practicing their sports, and honing their social skills. They were ready to conquer high school and all the opportunities it presented.

"Hey Clara, you ready for today?" Max asked, slinging his backpack over one shoulder.

"Yeah, I think so," Clara replied, managing a smile. "Just a bit nervous, you know?"

"Don't worry, you'll be great," Ash added, giving her a reassuring pat on the back. "We'll be there if you need us."

Their words comforted her, but she knew that high school was a vast, bustling place, and they wouldn't always be by her side.

THE INITIAL REACTIONS OF THEIR PEERS AND THE ATTENTION THEY RECEIVE

The Twins Quickly Gain Popularity with Their Charm and Athletic Abilities

As they walked through the school gates, Max and Ash immediately drew attention. Their confidence was palpable, and it didn't take long for them to start making new friends. They joined the football team tryouts and quickly impressed the coaches and fellow students with their skills. By lunchtime, they had already become the talk of the school, their names buzzing in the hallways.

Clara watched from a distance, a mix of pride and longing in her heart. She was happy for her brothers but couldn't help feeling the growing gap between them. Max and Ash were naturals at this, seamlessly blending into the high school scene, while she felt like an outsider looking in.

Clara Feels Proud of Her Brothers but Starts to Notice the Growing Gap Between Them

Throughout the day, Clara attended her classes, trying to focus on the subjects she loved. She had a passion for art and literature, finding solace in the creative expression they offered. However, every time she heard someone mention her brothers' names or saw them surrounded by new friends, a pang of loneliness struck her.

At lunch, she found a quiet corner in the cafeteria, pulling out her sketchbook to lose herself in drawing. She was working on a piece inspired by the school's architecture when she overheard a group of girls nearby talking about Max and Ash. Their admiration for her brothers was evident, and while it made her proud, it also highlighted her own struggles to find her place.

CLARA'S FEELINGS OF BEING OVERSHADOWED BY HER BROTHERS' POPULARITY

Clara's Struggle to Find Her Own Place in High School as She Feels Increasingly Overshadowed

In the following weeks, Clara's feelings of being overshadowed grew. Max and Ash were thriving, their popularity soaring with each passing day. They were invited to parties, joined various clubs, and were always surrounded by friends. Clara, on the other hand, found it challenging to break through the social barriers.

She tried joining the art club, hoping to connect with like-minded students who shared her passion. The club was welcoming, and she enjoyed the time spent painting and discussing art, but it didn't quite fill the void she felt. She also joined the literature club, finding comfort in the shared love for books and writing. However, despite her efforts, she often felt unnoticed, her brothers' shadows looming large over her.

Her Attempts to Join Clubs and Activities Where She Can Shine, Yet Feeling Unnoticed Compared to Her Brothers

Clara didn't give up. She continued to explore different clubs and activities, determined to find her niche. She signed up for the school newspaper, contributing her writing and illustrations. She attended various social events, trying to be more outgoing and make new friends. Yet, despite her efforts, she couldn't shake the feeling of being in the background.

One evening, Clara sat in her room, surrounded by her art supplies and notebooks. She felt a sense of frustration and sadness, wondering why it was so hard for her to find her place. Her brothers had it so easy, while she struggled to make a mark.

Her thoughts were interrupted by a knock on the door. It was Max.

"Hey, Clara," he said, sitting down beside her. "How are you holding up?"

Clara shrugged, not wanting to burden him with her feelings. "I'm okay, just tired."

Max looked at her with concern. "You know, you don't have to do this alone. If you ever need to talk or if you're feeling left out, we're here for you."

Clara appreciated his words, but deep down, she knew that she had to navigate her place in high school on her own. She needed to discover her strengths and passions, independent of her brothers' popularity.

As she lay in bed that night, Clara resolved to keep trying. She would continue to pursue her interests and connect with people who valued her for who she was. High school was a journey, and she was determined to find her own path, no matter how challenging it might be.

CHAPTER 2

THE RISE OF POPULARITY

MAX AND ASH'S GROWING POPULARITY AND THEIR RELATIONSHIPS WITH THEIR GIRLFRIENDS

The Twins' Social Lives Flourish as They Become Stars in Sports and Student Activities

Max and Ash's rise to popularity was meteoric. Within a few weeks, they had established themselves as stars on the football team, their athletic prowess earning them admiration from both peers and teachers. Max, with his outgoing nature, often led the charge, rallying the team and boosting morale. Ash, while slightly more reserved, showcased exceptional strategic thinking on the field, making him a valuable player and respected by his teammates.

Their involvement in student activities extended beyond sports. Max joined the student council, quickly becoming a charismatic leader who organized events and fostered school spirit. Ash became a member of the debate team, where his quick wit and sharp mind impressed everyone. Their success in these areas only added to their popularity, making them household names within the school.

Their Relationships with Popular Girls at School, Highlighting Their Charm and Social Prowess

As their social lives flourished, Max and Ash also caught the attention of some of the most popular girls in school. Max started dating Jessica, the head cheerleader, whose bubbly personality and infectious energy matched his own. They were often seen together, attending parties and school events, their relationship the talk of the school.

Ash, on the other hand, formed a connection with Emily, a talented musician known for her intelligence and grace. Their relationship was more subdued but no less significant. They bonded over their shared love for music and deep conversations, creating a strong emotional connection.

Both relationships highlighted the twins' charm and social prowess. Max and Jessica were the quintessential power couple, always in the spotlight, while Ash and Emily's quieter, more intellectual relationship showcased another side of popularity. Their girlfriends often joined them at social gatherings, further cementing their status as central figures in the school's social scene.

CLARA'S SENSE OF BEING LEFT OUT AND HER STRUGGLES TO FIT IN

Clara's Feelings of Loneliness as Her Brothers Get More Involved in Their Social Circles

While Max and Ash thrived, Clara found herself increasingly isolated. She watched as her brothers became the center of attention, their social circles expanding rapidly. She often felt like a shadow, unnoticed and unimportant compared to the twins. Her initial pride in their accomplishments gradually gave way to feelings of loneliness and self-doubt.

The more involved Max and Ash became in their social lives, the less time they seemed to have for Clara. They were always busy with practices, meetings, and outings with friends and girlfriends. Clara missed the close bond they once shared, feeling the sting of being left behind.

Her Efforts to Connect with Peers and Find Her Own Group of Friends

Despite her feelings of loneliness, Clara was determined to find her own place. She knew she had to take action if she wanted to overcome her sense of isolation. She joined the art club, where she could express her creativity and meet others who shared her passion. The club became a sanctuary for her, a place where she could be herself and escape the pressures of high school.

Clara also signed up for the school newspaper, contributing her writing and illustrations. She hoped this would be another avenue to connect with peers and showcase her talents. However, the newspaper staff was already a tight-knit group, and breaking into their circle proved challenging.

Undeterred, Clara continued to attend various social events, trying to be more outgoing and approachable. She made small talk with classmates, joined group projects, and attended school functions. Yet, despite her efforts, she often felt like an outsider looking in, her brothers' popularity casting a long shadow over her own attempts to fit in.

INTRODUCTION OF CLARA'S CLOSE FRIENDS: AMY, ALEX, AND MIA

Description of How Clara Meets Amy, Alex, and Mia, and the Bond They Form Over Shared Interests and Mutual Support

Clara's turning point came when she met Amy, Alex, and Mia in the art club. Amy was a quirky girl with a passion for photography. Her vibrant personality and unique perspective on life instantly intrigued Clara. Alex, a shy but incredibly talented painter, shared Clara's love for visual arts and quickly became a kindred spirit. Mia, a gifted writer, had a gentle demeanor and a knack for storytelling that resonated with Clara.

The four girls bonded over their shared interests and quickly formed a close-knit group. They spent countless hours together, working on art projects, discussing their favorite books, and supporting each other through the ups and downs of high school life. Their friendship provided Clara with the comfort and companionship she had been desperately seeking.

Amy, with her outgoing nature, often pulled Clara out of her shell, encouraging her to participate more actively in club activities and social events. Alex, understanding Clara's introverted tendencies, offered a quiet and supportive presence, always ready to listen and share her own experiences. Mia's thoughtful insights and empathetic nature made her a reliable confidante, someone Clara could trust with her deepest fears and hopes.

Their Role in Clara's Life as a Source of Comfort and Companionship

Amy, Alex, and Mia became Clara's pillars of support. They were there to celebrate her successes and lift her spirits when she felt down. They helped her navigate the complexities of high school, providing advice, laughter, and a sense of belonging. With their friendship, Clara began to feel less alone and more confident in her abilities and identity.

The girls often met at a local café after school, where they shared their latest creative endeavors and discussed everything from school drama to personal dreams. These meetings became a cherished routine, a safe space where Clara could express herself freely and be accepted for who she was.

CLARA MEETS ALEXANDER, WHO BECOMES HER BOYFRIEND AND A SOURCE OF SUPPORT

Clara's Growing Friendship with Alexander, a Kind and Understanding Boy Who Appreciates Her for Who She Is

It was during one of these art club meetings that Clara met Alexander, a kind-hearted and thoughtful boy with a passion for literature and history. Alexander was different from the other boys Clara knew. He was gentle, attentive, and genuinely interested in getting to know her.

Their friendship began with casual conversations about books and art. Alexander admired Clara's talent and sensitivity, and he often sought her opinion on his own writing projects. They spent hours discussing their favorite authors, sharing their creative processes, and exploring the depths of their imaginations.

Their Blossoming Relationship and How Alexander Becomes a Pillar of Support for Clara

As their friendship deepened, Clara found herself drawn to Alexander's warmth and understanding. He was always there to listen, offering thoughtful advice and unwavering support. Their connection grew stronger, and soon, their friendship blossomed into a romantic relationship.

Alexander became a steady presence in Clara's life, helping her navigate the challenges of high school with patience and care. He was there during her moments of self-doubt, reminding her of her worth and encouraging her to pursue her passions. His belief in her gave Clara the confidence to keep striving, even when the odds seemed against her.

They shared many special moments together, from quiet study sessions in the library to spontaneous dates exploring the city's art galleries. Alexander's support and love became a source of strength for Clara, helping her to see the beauty in herself and the world around her.

Reflection

Chapter 2 delves into the rise of Max and Ash's popularity and the resulting impact on Clara. While her brothers thrive in their social circles, Clara struggles to find her own place, feeling overshadowed and isolated. Through her determination and the support of her close friends and Alexander, Clara begins to carve out her own path, discovering the power of friendship and love in overcoming life's challenges. This chapter sets the stage for Clara's ongoing journey of self-discovery, resilience, and growth.

CHAPTER 3

THE BIRTHDAY PARTY INCIDENT

MAX AND ASH'S BIRTHDAY PARTY AND THEIR INSENSITIVITY TOWARDS CLARA

The Excitement and Preparation for the Twins' Big Birthday Bash, with All Their Friends Invited

Max and Ash's sixteenth birthday was a highly anticipated event. The twins had been planning their birthday bash for weeks, eager to make it the biggest and most memorable party of the year. Invitations had been sent out to almost everyone in their grade, promising a night of fun, music, and celebration.

The house was buzzing with activity on the day of the party. Decorations were being hung, food was being prepared, and a DJ was setting up in the backyard.

The twins were in their element, coordinating every detail to ensure everything went perfectly. Their friends started arriving early, filling the house with laughter and excitement.

Clara's Involvement in the Preparations, Hoping to Share in the Joy

Clara, despite her mixed feelings, wanted to be part of the celebration. She had always been close to her brothers, and she hoped that helping with the party preparations would bring them closer again. Clara spent the day assisting their parents with setting up the decorations, arranging the food, and making sure everything was in place. She even created a beautiful banner with her artistic skills, adding a personal touch to the festivities.

Clara's excitement was genuine, but there was also a lingering sense of unease. She hoped that tonight would be different, that her brothers would acknowledge her efforts and include her in their celebration. She longed to share in their joy and be part of their social circle, even if just for one night.

THE INCIDENT WHERE MAX AND ASH REVEAL CLARA'S BABY BLANKET, CAUSING HER EMBARRASSMENT

A Moment of Thoughtlessness When Max and Ash Expose Clara's Baby Blanket as a Joke

As the party was in full swing, the atmosphere was electric. The music was loud, the dance floor was packed, and everyone seemed to be having a great time. Max and Ash, enjoying the attention and the success of their party, were in high spirits. They moved through the crowd, mingling with friends and soaking up the admiration.

In the midst of the revelry, someone brought up childhood memories, and the conversation turned to embarrassing moments. Max, in a moment of thoughtless excitement, remembered Clara's old baby blanket. He had seen it recently when they were cleaning out the attic and thought it would be a funny story to share.

"Hey, guys, you won't believe what we found the other day," Max called out, his voice carrying over the music. "Clara's old baby blanket! She still has it!"

Ash, caught up in the moment, chimed in. "Yeah, she used to carry it everywhere. We should show them!"

Before Clara could react, Max dashed upstairs and returned with the blanket. He held it up for everyone to see, laughing as he recounted stories from their childhood. The crowd joined in, laughing and making playful comments. To Max and Ash, it was a harmless joke, a way to lighten the mood and share a laugh. But for Clara, it was a nightmare.

Clara's Immediate Reaction of Humiliation and Hurt, Feeling Betrayed by Her Brothers

Clara's heart sank as she saw Max holding up her baby blanket. Her face flushed with embarrassment, and she felt a knot form in her stomach. The laughter and teasing from the crowd felt like daggers, each one piercing her already fragile self-esteem. She looked at her brothers, hoping they would realize their mistake and stop, but they were too caught up in the moment to notice her distress.

Tears welled up in Clara's eyes as she stood frozen, unable to move or speak. The room seemed to close in around her, the laughter echoing in her ears. She felt a deep sense of betrayal, unable to comprehend how her brothers could be so insensitive. The baby blanket was a private piece of her childhood, a source of comfort and security, and now it was being ridiculed in front of everyone.

Overwhelmed by humiliation and hurt, Clara couldn't take it anymore. She turned and fled the room, her vision blurred by tears. She heard someone call her name, but she didn't stop. She ran upstairs to her room, slamming the door shut behind her.

CLARA'S EMOTIONAL RESPONSE AND HER DECISION TO ISOLATE HERSELF

Clara's Retreat to Her Room, Overwhelmed with Embarrassment and Sadness

In the safety of her room, Clara collapsed onto her bed, clutching her baby blanket tightly. She sobbed uncontrollably, the events of the night replaying in her mind. The sense of betrayal and humiliation was overwhelming. She had wanted so badly to be part of her brothers' celebration, to feel included and appreciated. Instead, she felt like the butt of a cruel joke.

Clara's emotions were a whirlwind of sadness, anger, and confusion. She couldn't understand why Max and Ash had done this to her. Did they think so little of her? Did they not care about her feelings? These questions swirled in her mind, deepening her sense of isolation.

Her Decision to Withdraw from Her Brothers and Their Friends, Leading to a Period of Isolation

The next day, Clara couldn't bear to face her brothers or their friends. The thought of going to school and seeing everyone who had laughed at her was unbearable. She decided to stay in her room, avoiding any contact with Max and Ash. Her parents noticed her absence and tried to comfort her, but Clara couldn't bring herself to talk about what had happened.

Days turned into weeks, and Clara's isolation grew. She withdrew from her brothers, barely speaking to them unless absolutely necessary. She stopped attending social events, avoiding any situation where she might run into their friends. Even at school, she kept to herself, choosing solitary activities over group ones.

Her once vibrant spirit dulled, and she found solace in her art and writing, using them as an outlet for her pain. Her friends, Amy, Alex, and Mia, noticed the change in her and tried to reach out, but Clara found it hard to open up. The humiliation she had felt was too deep, and the trust she had lost in her brothers too significant to easily mend.

Clara's decision to isolate herself marked the beginning of a difficult period. She struggled with feelings of inadequacy and loneliness, questioning her worth and her place in the world. The incident at the birthday party had shattered her confidence, and it would take time, support, and inner strength to rebuild it.

Reflection

Chapter 3 captures a pivotal moment in Clara's life. The birthday party incident, driven by Max and Ash's thoughtlessness, leads to a deep sense of betrayal and humiliation for Clara. Her emotional response and subsequent isolation highlight the challenges she faces in rebuilding her self-esteem and finding her place. This chapter sets the stage for Clara's journey of healing, self-discovery, and eventual reconciliation, marking a significant turning point in her story.

CHAPTER 4

THE AFTERMATH

THE FALLOUT FROM THE PARTY AND CLARA BEING BULLIED AT SCHOOL

The Rumors and Teasing That Follow Clara at School, Exacerbating Her Feelings of Isolation

The morning after the party, Clara's worst fears came true. As soon as she stepped onto the school grounds, she could feel the eyes on her. Whispers and giggles followed her down the hallways, and she overheard snippets of conversations that made her heart sink.

"Did you hear about Clara and her baby blanket?"

"I can't believe she still has it. How embarrassing!"

"She must be so childish. No wonder she's so quiet."

Clara tried to keep her head down, focusing on getting to her classes without drawing more attention to herself. But the rumors and teasing were relentless. Some students made snide comments as she passed by, while others outright laughed in her face. The humiliation from the party had spilled over into her school life, turning it into a daily ordeal.

Her Struggle to Face Her Peers and the Impact on Her Self-Esteem

Facing her peers became an excruciating task. Clara felt a constant knot of anxiety in her stomach, dreading every interaction and fearing further humiliation. She often arrived at school early to avoid the crowds and stayed in the classroom during breaks to minimize contact with others. The vibrant, confident girl she once was seemed to fade away, replaced by a shadow of her former self.

Her self-esteem took a severe hit. Clara started to believe the cruel words whispered behind her back. She questioned her worth and felt undeserving of friendship or respect. Her academic performance began to suffer as her concentration waned, and the subjects she once loved felt like a burden.

CLARA'S TRANSFORMATION: CHANGING HER HAIR TO BLACK, DRESSING IN BLACK, AND BECOMING WITHDRAWN

Clara's Outward Transformation as a Way to Cope with Her Pain and Create a Barrier Between Herself and the World

In an attempt to protect herself from further pain, Clara decided to change her appearance. She dyed her hair jet black, a stark contrast to her natural auburn locks. The dark color felt like a shield, a way to distance herself from the person she used to be and the vulnerability she had shown.

She also began to dress in black, favoring oversized hoodies, jeans, and boots. The somber attire reflected her inner turmoil and served as a barrier between her and the world. It was a statement of her desire to be left alone, to not be seen or judged. Her new look drew curious glances, but it also kept people at a distance, which was exactly what Clara wanted.

Her Withdrawal from Social Activities and Focus on Her Inner World

Clara withdrew from all social activities. She stopped attending art club meetings, skipped school events, and avoided any situation that required interaction with her peers. The once lively and engaged student became a solitary figure, always on the periphery, watching but never participating.

Her room became her sanctuary, a place where she could escape from the harsh reality of school life. She spent hours drawing, writing, and listening to music. Her art took on darker themes, reflecting her pain and loneliness. Writing became a cathartic outlet, allowing her to express emotions she couldn't articulate in person.

THE IMPACT OF THIS PERIOD ON HER SELF-ESTEEM AND MENTAL HEALTH

The Deepening of Clara's Emotional Struggles, Including Anxiety and Depression

Clara's emotional struggles deepened as the weeks turned into months. The anxiety that had started with the bullying grew into a constant companion. She found it difficult to sleep, her mind racing with thoughts of the day's events and the dread of what tomorrow might bring. The once simple act of walking into school felt like climbing a mountain, her heart pounding with fear and anticipation of ridicule.

Depression settled in as well. Clara felt an overwhelming sense of hopelessness and sadness. She lost interest in activities she once enjoyed, including her art and writing. The days blurred together, each one feeling like a struggle just to get through. Her interactions with her family became strained as she withdrew further into herself, unable to share the depth of her pain.

Her Reliance on Her Close Friends and Alexander, Who Try to Support Her Through This Difficult Time

Despite her withdrawal, Clara's close friends and Alexander remained a lifeline. Amy, Alex, and Mia noticed the changes in Clara and reached out to her, refusing to let her isolation push them away. They visited her at home, brought her favorite snacks, and tried to coax her out of her room. They offered a listening ear and a shoulder to cry on, understanding that Clara needed time to heal but also that she needed their presence.

Alexander, more than anyone, became Clara's rock. He spent countless hours with her, talking, listening, and just being there. He didn't push her to talk about her feelings but made it clear that he was always ready to listen. He supported her in small ways, like helping with homework, bringing over movies to watch together, and even just sitting in comfortable silence.

One evening, as they sat in Clara's room, Alexander gently took her hand. "Clara, I know this is hard, and I can't imagine how you're feeling. But I want you to know that you're not alone. We're all here for you, and we'll get through this together."

His words brought a flicker of hope to Clara's heart. She squeezed his hand, grateful for his unwavering support. It was moments like these that gave her the strength to keep going, even when everything felt so bleak.

Reflection

Chapter 4 delves into the aftermath of the birthday party incident, highlighting the severe impact on Clara's mental and emotional well-being. The bullying at school exacerbates her feelings of isolation and humiliation, leading to a dramatic transformation as she withdraws from social activities. Despite the darkness of this period, the support of her close friends and Alexander provides a glimmer of hope, setting the stage for Clara's journey toward healing and self-discovery. This chapter underscores the themes of resilience and the importance of support systems in overcoming personal challenges.

CHAPTER 5
FINDING HER PATH

CLARA'S JOURNEY TOWARDS SELF-DISCOVERY AND HEALING

Clara's Gradual Realization That She Needs to Reclaim Her Identity and Find Her Own Path

Clara's journey towards self-discovery began with small, subtle changes. After months of isolation and introspection, she started to realize that she couldn't continue living in the shadows of her pain and fear. The turning point came during a quiet evening when she was alone in her room, surrounded by her sketches and journals. She looked at her artwork, seeing not just the darkness and despair but also glimpses of hope and resilience.

She began to understand that reclaiming her identity meant embracing both her strengths and her vulnerabilities. Clara made a conscious decision to start rebuilding herself, piece by piece. She started by revisiting the things that once brought her joy, rediscovering her love for art and literature. She decided to face her fears and take control of her narrative, rather than letting the events of the past define her.

Her Exploration of Interests and Passions That Bring Her Joy and a Sense of Purpose

Clara immersed herself in her creative pursuits. She began by setting small goals, such as completing a sketchbook or writing a short story. Each accomplishment, no matter how minor, boosted her confidence and reignited her passion. She found solace in painting, where she could express her emotions without words. The colors and strokes on the canvas became a reflection of her inner world, a place where she could process her experiences and heal.

Writing became another powerful outlet for Clara. She started journaling daily, documenting her thoughts, feelings, and progress. Through writing, she could articulate her pain, explore her dreams, and envision a future beyond her current struggles. The act of putting pen to paper helped her make sense of her emotions and gave her a sense of control over her life.

As she explored her interests, Clara also began to step out of her comfort zone. She attended art workshops and writing seminars, where she met people who shared her passions. These new connections provided her with a supportive community and further encouraged her to pursue her creative endeavors. The encouragement and feedback she received from these groups played a crucial role in her healing process.

HER INTEREST IN THERAPY AND WRITING AS A WAY TO COPE WITH HER EXPERIENCES

Clara's Discovery of the Therapeutic Power of Writing and Her Decision to Pursue It Seriously

Clara's journaling evolved from a personal coping mechanism into a serious pursuit. She realized that writing had a therapeutic power that could not only help her but also others who might be going through similar experiences. Inspired by this realization, Clara began to research the benefits of writing therapy and how it could be used as a tool for healing.

She started writing essays and articles about her journey, sharing her insights and the lessons she had learned. Her writing resonated with many, and she received messages of support and gratitude from readers who found solace in her words. This positive feedback encouraged Clara to continue writing and to consider it as a potential career path.

Her Interest in Psychology and Therapy as a Career Path, Inspired by Her Own Experiences

In parallel with her writing, Clara developed a keen interest in psychology. Her experiences with bullying, isolation, and emotional turmoil had given her a deep understanding of mental health issues. She wanted to help others who were struggling, just as she had been helped by her friends, family, and her own creative outlets.

Clara began to read extensively about psychology, therapy, and counseling. She was fascinated by the human mind and the ways in which people could heal from trauma and build resilience. This newfound passion led her to consider a career in therapy, where she could combine her understanding of psychology with her desire to help others.

GRADUATION AND CLARA'S DECISION TO PURSUE A CAREER AS A THERAPIST AND WRITER

Clara's Academic Achievements and the Sense of Accomplishment as She Graduates High School

As Clara approached her senior year of high school, she focused on her academic goals with renewed determination. She excelled in her classes, particularly in subjects related to psychology and literature. Her hard work paid off, and she graduated with honors, a testament to her resilience and dedication.

Graduation day was a significant milestone for Clara. It marked the end of a challenging chapter and the beginning of a new, hopeful one. As she walked across the stage to receive her diploma, she felt a profound sense of accomplishment. She had overcome immense obstacles and emerged stronger and more self-assured.

Her Decision to Study Psychology in College and to Continue Developing Her Writing

With high school behind her, Clara was ready to embark on the next phase of her journey. She decided to pursue a degree in psychology, enrolling at a university known for its strong psychology program.

Clara was excited to deepen her understanding of the human mind and to learn how to support others in their healing journeys.

At the same time, Clara was determined to continue developing her writing. She enrolled in creative writing courses and joined the university's literary magazine, where she could hone her skills and share her work with a broader audience. Writing remained a central part of her life, a source of joy, and a powerful tool for self-expression and connection.

Throughout college, Clara balanced her academic studies with her creative pursuits. She worked diligently in her psychology classes, eager to absorb knowledge and gain practical experience. Her writing flourished, and she published several essays and short stories, gaining recognition for her insightful and heartfelt work.

Reflection

Chapter 5 highlights Clara's path to self-discovery and healing. Through art, writing, and a newfound interest in psychology, Clara begins to reclaim her identity and find her purpose. Her academic achievements and decision to pursue a career as a therapist and writer mark significant steps in her journey. This chapter underscores the importance of resilience, self-expression, and the pursuit of passions in overcoming challenges and building a fulfilling life. Clara's story continues to inspire as she navigates her path with courage and determination, setting the stage for further growth and success.

CHAPTER 6

RECONCILIATION

CLARA'S PROGRESS IN HER CAREER AND PERSONAL GROWTH OVER THE YEARS

Clara's Journey Through College, Her Success in Her Studies, and the Beginning of Her Career as a Therapist and Writer

Clara's college years were transformative. She immersed herself in her psychology studies, fascinated by the intricacies of the human mind and the therapeutic techniques that could help heal emotional wounds. Her professors recognized her dedication and intellect, often praising her insightful contributions in class. Clara's passion for understanding mental health and supporting others drove her to excel academically.

In addition to her studies, Clara continued to nurture her love for writing. She wrote for the university's literary magazine, sharing her experiences and reflections on overcoming adversity. Her articles resonated with many readers, and she soon gained a following for her poignant and authentic voice. Clara also participated in writing workshops and competitions, further honing her skills and expanding her repertoire.

Upon graduation, Clara pursued a dual career path as both a therapist and a writer. She secured a position at a well-regarded mental health clinic, where she began to apply her knowledge and skills to help clients navigate their own challenges. Clara found immense fulfillment in her work, knowing that she was making a positive impact on people's lives.

Her writing career flourished simultaneously. Clara published several essays and short stories in prominent literary journals, and she even secured a book deal for a memoir that chronicled her journey from pain to healing. Her memoir was met with critical acclaim, praised for its raw honesty and inspiring message.

Her Personal Growth and the Development of Her Self-Confidence and Sense of Purpose

Clara's professional achievements were paralleled by significant personal growth. Through her experiences in college and her early career, she developed a strong sense of self-confidence and purpose. Clara no longer saw herself as a victim of her past but as a survivor who had emerged stronger and more resilient.

She built a network of supportive friends and colleagues who admired her strength and integrity. Clara also deepened her relationship with Alexander, who remained a steadfast presence in her life. Their bond grew stronger as they navigated the challenges and triumphs of adulthood together.

Clara's sense of purpose was clear: she was dedicated to helping others heal and find their own paths to happiness. Her work as a therapist and writer allowed her to fulfill this mission, and she found great joy in the process. Clara's journey had transformed her into a confident, compassionate, and empowered woman.

MAX AND ASH'S REALIZATION OF THEIR PAST MISTAKES AND THEIR EFFORTS TO MAKE AMENDS

The Twins' Growing Maturity and Their Recognition of How Their Actions Had Hurt Clara

As the years passed, Max and Ash matured significantly. Their high school days were behind them, and they had both pursued their own careers and interests. Max became a successful chef, while Ash followed his passion for hospitality management. Despite their successes, both brothers carried a lingering sense of guilt about how they had treated Clara during their teenage years.

Through conversations with their parents and personal reflection, Max and Ash began to fully grasp the impact of their actions on Clara. They realized that their thoughtless behavior had caused her deep pain and isolation, and they felt a profound sense of regret. This awareness prompted them to reach out to Clara, hoping to make amends and rebuild their relationship.

Their Attempts to Reach Out to Clara, Express Their Regret, and Seek Her Forgiveness

Max and Ash decided to take the first step by reaching out to Clara with heartfelt letters. They each wrote to her, expressing their remorse and acknowledging the hurt they had caused. They shared how much they had grown and changed, and how deeply they regretted their insensitivity.

In his letter, Max wrote, "Clara, I am truly sorry for the pain I caused you during our high school years. I was immature and thoughtless, and I didn't realize how my actions affected you. I hope you can find it in your heart to forgive me and allow us to rebuild our bond as siblings."

Ash's letter echoed similar sentiments. "Clara, I regret not being there for you when you needed us the most. I have spent a lot of time reflecting on our past, and I am deeply sorry for my role in your suffering. I want to make things right and show you that I have grown and learned from my mistakes."

The letters marked the beginning of their efforts to reconnect with Clara. They also reached out to her in person, inviting her to spend time with them and their families. Max and Ash were determined to show

Clara through their actions that they had changed and were committed to being better brothers.

THE HEARTFELT APOLOGY FROM HER BROTHERS AND CLARA'S DECISION TO FORGIVE THEM

A Poignant Family Moment Where Max and Ash Apologize Sincerely to Clara

The opportunity for a face-to-face apology came during a family gathering. Clara, Max, Ash, and their parents were all present, creating a supportive environment for this crucial conversation. Max and Ash had prepared for this moment, hoping to convey their sincerity and regret.

As the family sat together in the living room, Max and Ash took turns speaking. They reiterated the apologies from their letters, adding more heartfelt words about their love for Clara and their desire to mend their relationship. Tears were shed as they spoke, their voices filled with emotion.

"Clara," Max said, his voice trembling, "we were terrible brothers to you, and I am so sorry for the pain we caused. You deserved so much better from us. Please forgive us."

Ash added, "We understand if it takes time for you to trust us again. We just want you to know how deeply sorry we are and that we are committed to being the brothers you deserve."

Clara's Decision to Forgive Her Brothers, Understanding That They Have Grown and Changed

Clara listened to her brothers' apologies, her heart heavy with the weight of their words. She saw the sincerity in their eyes and heard the genuine remorse in their voices. For years, she had carried the pain of their actions, but now, faced with their heartfelt apologies, she felt a shift within herself.

Clara took a deep breath and spoke, her voice steady but filled with emotion. "Max, Ash, your actions hurt me deeply, and it took me a long time to heal from that pain. But I can see that you have both grown and changed. I forgive you, not just for your sake, but for mine as well. Holding onto the past only holds us back. I want us to move forward together, as a family."

Tears filled the room as Clara's words brought a sense of relief and hope. The family embraced, feeling the healing power of forgiveness and reconciliation. Clara's decision to forgive her brothers was a testament to her strength and her commitment to moving forward with love and compassion.

Reflection

Chapter 6 highlights the theme of reconciliation. Clara's progress in her career and personal growth sets the stage for healing old wounds. Max and Ash's realization of their past mistakes and their sincere efforts to make amends lead to a poignant moment of apology and forgiveness. This chapter underscores the importance of maturity, understanding, and the power of forgiveness in healing relationships and moving forward. Clara's journey continues to inspire, showing that even the deepest wounds can be healed with love, growth, and compassion.

CHAPTER 7

A NEW CHAPTER

CLARA'S CONTINUED RELATIONSHIP WITH ALEXANDER, WHO HAS BEEN A STEADFAST SUPPORT

Clara and Alexander's Deepening Relationship, Built on Mutual Respect, Love, and Support

Throughout the years, Clara and Alexander's relationship deepened into a bond that was unbreakable. Alexander had been Clara's rock during some of the most challenging times of her life, offering her unwavering support and understanding. Their relationship was built on a foundation of mutual respect, love, and shared values.

Alexander admired Clara's resilience and her dedication to helping others through her work as a therapist. He was proud of her accomplishments as a writer, often being the first to read her new pieces and offering thoughtful feedback. In turn, Clara supported Alexander in his own endeavors, encouraging him in his career and personal growth.

Their relationship was characterized by open communication and a deep sense of trust. They had learned to navigate life's challenges together, always prioritizing each other's happiness and well-being. Clara and Alexander found joy in the simple moments they shared, whether it was cooking dinner together, taking long walks, or just sitting quietly, enjoying each other's company.

Their Decision to Get Married, Celebrating Their Journey Together

As their relationship grew stronger, Clara and Alexander began to talk about their future together. They both knew that they wanted to spend the rest of their lives with each other, and the idea of marriage felt like a natural next step. One evening, during a quiet dinner at their favorite restaurant, Alexander proposed.

He took Clara's hand, looking into her eyes with a mixture of love and anticipation. "Clara, you are the most incredible person I've ever known. You've brought so much joy and meaning into my life. Will you marry me?"

Clara felt tears of happiness well up in her eyes as she nodded, her heart swelling with love. "Yes, Alexander. I can't imagine my life without you."

Their engagement was a time of celebration and excitement. They planned their wedding together, wanting it to reflect their journey and their love for each other. Clara chose a beautiful, rustic venue that reminded her of the peaceful countryside where she often found inspiration for her writing. They invited their closest family and friends, eager to share their special day with the people who had supported them throughout their relationship.

THEIR MARRIAGE AND THE BEGINNING OF THEIR FAMILY LIFE

The Joyous Wedding of Clara and Alexander, Surrounded by Family and Friends

The day of the wedding was filled with joy and emotion. The venue was adorned with flowers and lights, creating a magical atmosphere that perfectly captured the essence of Clara and Alexander's love. As Clara walked down the aisle, she felt an overwhelming sense of gratitude and happiness. Her parents, Max, Ash, and her friends beamed with pride, knowing how far she had come.

Alexander stood at the altar, his eyes shining with love as he watched Clara approach. Their vows were heartfelt and sincere, each word a testament to their journey and their commitment to each other. "Clara," Alexander said, his voice steady but filled with emotion, "I promise to love you, support you, and stand by your side, no matter what life brings. You are my heart, my inspiration, and my forever."

Clara's voice trembled with emotion as she responded, "Alexander, you are my rock and my soulmate. I promise to cherish you, to grow with you, and to love you unconditionally. Together, we can face anything."

The ceremony was followed by a lively reception, filled with laughter, dancing, and heartfelt toasts. Clara and Alexander's friends and family shared stories, celebrating the couple's love and the beautiful life they were building together. The day was a perfect reflection of their love story, filled with joy, gratitude, and the promise of a bright future.

The Beginning of Their Life Together as a Married Couple, Filled with Love and Partnership

After their wedding, Clara and Alexander settled into their life as a married couple. They created a home filled with love, laughter, and mutual respect. Their partnership was strong, built on the foundation of their shared experiences and their unwavering support for each other.

They continued to pursue their individual passions while always making time for each other. Clara's career as a therapist and writer flourished, and Alexander excelled in his field, supported by Clara's encouragement. They made a point to celebrate each other's achievements and to be there for each other during challenging times.

Their home was a place of warmth and comfort, where they could unwind and enjoy each other's company. They cherished the simple routines of married life, from cooking meals together to taking weekend trips. Their love for each other only grew stronger with time, and they often marveled at how lucky they were to have found one another.

CLARA AND ALEXANDER'S THREE CHILDREN: ERIC, GINNY, AND GEORGIA

The Birth of Their Three Children and the Happiness They Bring to Clara and Alexander's Life

Clara and Alexander's joy multiplied with the arrival of their three children: Eric, Ginny, and Georgia. Each child brought a new dimension of love and happiness into their lives, filling their home with laughter and adventure.

Eric, their firstborn, was a curious and imaginative child, always eager to explore and learn. He inherited Clara's love for books and storytelling, often creating elaborate tales to share with his family. Ginny, their second child, was a spirited and energetic girl with a passion for music and dance. Her joyful presence and creative spirit brought light to everyone around her. Georgia, the youngest, was a gentle and thoughtful child, with a deep love for nature and animals. She had a calming presence and a heart full of empathy.

Clara and Alexander embraced the challenges and joys of parenthood with open hearts. They found immense fulfillment in raising their children, guiding them with love and patience. Each milestone, from first steps to school achievements, was celebrated with pride and joy.

The Loving and Nurturing Environment Clara and Alexander Create for Their Children

Clara and Alexander were committed to creating a loving and nurturing environment for their children. They encouraged Eric, Ginny, and Georgia to pursue their passions and to express themselves freely. Their home was filled with creativity, with art supplies, musical instruments, and books available for the children to explore their interests.

Family time was a priority, and they spent weekends on outdoor adventures, visiting museums, and engaging in activities that fostered learning and bonding. Clara often shared her love for art and writing with her children, while Alexander introduced them to his interests and hobbies.

Their parenting style was rooted in love, respect, and open communication. Clara and Alexander made sure to listen to their children's thoughts and feelings, offering guidance and support while allowing them to grow into their own unique individuals. Their home was a safe haven, where the children knew they were loved and valued.

Reflection

Chapter 7 showcases the beautiful evolution of Clara and Alexander's relationship, culminating in their joyous wedding and the beginning of their family life. The birth of their three children, Eric, Ginny, and Georgia, brings even more happiness and fulfillment into their lives. Clara and Alexander's commitment to creating a loving and nurturing environment for their family highlights the enduring themes of love, partnership, and the importance of a supportive and caring home. This chapter reflects the culmination of Clara's journey, from overcoming past challenges to building a life filled with love, joy, and purpose.

CHAPTER 8

HAPPILY EVER AFTER

CLARA'S SUCCESSFUL CAREER AND FULFILLING FAMILY LIFE

Clara's Achievements as a Therapist and Writer, Making a Positive Impact on Others Through Her Work

Clara's career continued to flourish as she established herself as a respected therapist and an acclaimed writer. Her work at the mental health clinic earned her a reputation for her empathetic approach and her ability to connect deeply with her clients. Clara's unique blend of professional knowledge and personal experience allowed her to offer profound insights and support to those seeking help. Her clients often spoke of how she helped them navigate their struggles, providing them with tools and encouragement to heal and grow.

In addition to her therapy practice, Clara's writing career reached new heights. Her memoir became a bestseller, resonating with readers worldwide who found solace and inspiration in her story. Clara continued to write essays and articles for various publications, sharing her journey and the lessons she had learned. Her words touched countless lives, offering hope and motivation to those facing similar challenges.

Clara also conducted workshops and seminars, blending her skills as a therapist and a writer to educate and inspire others. She often spoke at conferences, sharing her expertise on topics such as resilience, mental health, and the healing power of creativity. Clara's impact extended beyond her immediate community, reaching a global audience through her written and spoken words.

The Balance She Finds Between Her Career and Her Role as a Mother and Wife

Despite her demanding career, Clara always prioritized her family. She skillfully balanced her professional responsibilities with her roles as a mother and a wife. Clara's ability to manage her time effectively allowed her to be present for her children and her husband while still pursuing her passions.

Mornings in the household were a blend of bustling activity and cherished routines. Clara ensured that breakfast was a time for family connection, where they discussed their plans for the day and shared moments of laughter. After dropping the kids off at school, she would head to her clinic, ready to immerse herself in her work.

Clara's evenings were dedicated to her family. She helped Eric with his homework, listened to Ginny practice her latest dance routine, and explored nature with Georgia. Dinner was a sacred family time, where they gathered to enjoy a meal and discuss their day. Clara and Alexander also made it a point to have regular date nights, nurturing their relationship and ensuring they remained connected.

Weekends were filled with family adventures and creative activities. Clara often took the children on outings to museums, parks, and libraries, fostering their curiosity and love for learning. She and Alexander worked as a team, supporting each other in their parenting roles and maintaining a harmonious household.

THE STRONG BOND BETWEEN CLARA AND HER BROTHERS, NOW HEALED AND STRENGTHENED BY THEIR EXPERIENCES

The Deepened Relationship Between Clara, Max, and Ash, Forged Through Understanding and Forgiveness

Over the years, the bond between Clara, Max, and Ash deepened significantly. The process of reconciliation had brought them closer, and their relationship was now built on a foundation of understanding, respect, and unconditional love. The shared experiences and the journey of healing had transformed their sibling dynamic, making it stronger and more resilient.

Max and Ash admired Clara's strength and achievements, often expressing their pride in her. They made a conscious effort to stay involved in each other's lives, celebrating milestones and supporting one another through challenges. Family gatherings were filled with warmth and laughter, as they reminisced about their past and created new memories together.

Max, who had become a successful chef, often sought Clara's advice on matters related to work-life balance. Ash, who excelled in hospitality management, shared his innovative projects with Clara, appreciating her insights and encouragement. The three siblings enjoyed spending time together, whether it was a casual brunch, a holiday celebration, or a spontaneous family trip.

The Support and Love They Share as Siblings, Cherishing Their Family Bond

The bond between Clara, Max, and Ash extended to their respective families as well. Their children grew up together, forming close relationships and enjoying the benefits of a loving extended family. The cousins often played together, creating a lively and joyful atmosphere during family gatherings.

Max and Ash were also supportive of Clara's children, attending their school events and celebrating their achievements. Clara reciprocated by being an involved and loving aunt, always ready to offer her support and guidance. The extended family cherished their bond, understanding the importance of maintaining strong connections and supporting each other through life's ups and downs.

Family traditions became an integral part of their lives. They celebrated holidays together, with each sibling contributing to the festivities in their own unique way. They also established an annual family reunion, a time when they could all come together, reconnect, and reflect on the journey they had traveled as a family.

REFLECTIONS ON THE JOURNEY AND THE LESSONS LEARNED ABOUT FORGIVENESS, RESILIENCE, AND THE IMPORTANCE OF FAMILY

Clara's Reflections on Her Journey, Recognizing the Strength She Found Within Herself and the Importance of Family

As Clara looked back on her journey, she felt a profound sense of gratitude and accomplishment. She recognized the immense strength she had found within herself, a strength that had carried her through the darkest times and guided her toward healing and growth. Clara was proud of the woman she had become, someone who had transformed pain into purpose and used her experiences to help others.

Clara often reflected on the pivotal moments that had shaped her life. The support of her friends, the unwavering love of Alexander, and the reconciliation with her brothers were all key elements in her story. She understood that her journey was not just about her own resilience but also about the collective strength and love of her family.

The Lessons of Forgiveness, Resilience, and Unconditional Love That Have Shaped Her Life

The lessons Clara had learned were profound and enduring. Forgiveness had been a crucial part of her healing process, allowing her to release the pain of the past and embrace a brighter future. She understood that forgiveness was not about condoning the actions that had hurt her but about freeing herself from the burden of resentment and anger.

Resilience was another key lesson. Clara had learned that resilience was not about being invulnerable but about having the courage to face challenges, adapt, and grow stronger. Her journey had taught her the importance of self-compassion, patience, and the willingness to seek help when needed.

Unconditional love was the foundation of Clara's life. The love she shared with her family and friends had been a source of strength and inspiration. Clara believed that unconditional love was about accepting others for who they were, supporting them through their struggles, and celebrating their successes.

Clara's reflections were often captured in her writing, where she shared her insights and experiences with a broader audience. Her words continued to inspire others, offering hope and guidance to those on their own journeys of healing and growth.

Reflection

Chapter 8 concludes with a celebration of Clara's successful career, fulfilling family life, and the strong bonds she shares with her siblings. Her reflections on forgiveness, resilience, and unconditional love highlight the lessons she has learned and the strength she has found within herself. Clara's journey is a testament to the power of healing, growth, and the enduring importance of family. Her story continues to inspire, showing that even in the face of adversity, it is possible to find happiness, purpose, and a happily ever after.

CHAPTER 9

FINAL THOUGHTS

THE STORY CONCLUDES WITH A REFLECTION ON CLARA'S JOURNEY FROM BEING OVERSHADOWED AND HURT TO FINDING HER OWN PATH AND HAPPINESS

A Final Reflection on Clara's Growth, from a Young Girl Overshadowed by Her Brothers to a Confident Woman Who Has Found Her Own Path

As Clara sat in her cozy study, looking out at the garden where her children played, she allowed herself a moment of quiet reflection. Her life had been a remarkable journey of growth and transformation. She thought back to her early years, feeling overshadowed by her brothers, Max and Ash. Those days were filled with the insecurities and struggles of a young girl trying to find her place in a world that seemed to favor others over her.

Clara remembered the pivotal moments that had shaped her path: the painful experiences of high school, the feeling of isolation, and the transformative power of art and writing that had helped her heal. She recalled the support of her close friends and Alexander, who had been her pillars of strength. Each challenge she had faced had forged her into the woman she had become.

Today, Clara stood as a confident and accomplished woman. She had built a successful career as a therapist and writer, impacting countless lives with her empathy, wisdom, and creativity. Her personal journey had transformed her pain into purpose, allowing her to help others navigate their own struggles. Clara had found her voice and her path, no longer overshadowed but shining brightly in her own right.

The Happiness and Fulfillment She Has Achieved Through Her Perseverance and Self-Discovery

The happiness Clara felt was not just a fleeting emotion but a deep, enduring sense of fulfillment. Her life was rich with love, purpose, and contentment.

The balance she had found between her professional achievements and her roles as a wife and mother brought her immense joy.

Clara's perseverance had paid off. She had pursued her passions relentlessly, even when the road was tough. Her dedication to her work as a therapist allowed her to touch lives and make a real difference. The stories she wrote and shared resonated with people from all walks of life, offering them hope and encouragement.

Her family was her greatest source of happiness. Watching her children, Eric, Ginny, and Georgia, grow and thrive filled her with pride and love. Her relationship with Alexander remained a cornerstone of her life, built on mutual respect, love, and unwavering support. The deep bonds she had with her brothers, now healed and strengthened, added to the sense of completeness and belonging she felt.

EMPHASIS ON THE THEMES OF PERSONAL GROWTH, RECONCILIATION, AND THE ENDURING POWER OF LOVE AND FAMILY

**The Enduring Themes of the Story: The Power of Personal Growth, the Importance of

Reconciliation, and the Lasting Strength of Love and Family

Clara's story was a testament to the power of personal growth. Her journey highlighted the importance of self-discovery, resilience, and the courage to face one's fears. Clara had shown that growth often comes from the most challenging experiences and that it is possible to transform pain into strength and purpose.

Reconciliation was another key theme. The healing of her relationship with Max and Ash had been a crucial part of Clara's journey. It demonstrated that forgiveness is a powerful tool for healing, not just for those who are forgiven but for those who forgive. The renewed bond between the siblings was a source of joy and support, proving that it is never too late to mend relationships and build a better future together.

The lasting strength of love and family was at the heart of Clara's story. Her family had been her foundation, providing her with the support and love she needed to overcome her struggles. The love she shared with Alexander, her children, and her brothers was a testament to the enduring power of family bonds. It was a reminder that, despite life's challenges, love and family can offer the strength and resilience needed to thrive.

A Hopeful and Inspiring Message About the Transformative Power of Love and Forgiveness

Clara's journey carried a hopeful and inspiring message. It showed that love and forgiveness have the power to transform lives. Through love, Clara found the strength to face her challenges and the courage to pursue her dreams. Through forgiveness, she healed old wounds and built stronger, more meaningful relationships.

Her story was a beacon of hope for anyone facing adversity. It demonstrated that no matter how dark the past, it is possible to find light and happiness. Clara's life was a testament to the idea that we all have the power to shape our destinies, to find our paths, and to create lives filled with love, purpose, and fulfillment.

Conclusion

As the story of Clara's journey comes to a close, it leaves readers with a profound sense of hope and inspiration. Clara's transformation from a young girl overshadowed and hurt to a confident woman who found her path and happiness is a powerful narrative of personal growth, reconciliation, and the enduring power of love and family. Her story reminds us that, with perseverance, resilience, and the support of loved ones, we can overcome any obstacle and create a life filled with joy and fulfillment. Clara's journey is a testament to the transformative power of love and forgiveness, offering a timeless message of hope for all.

PART THREE

CLARA'S PROFESSIONAL AND PERSONAL JOURNEY AND DEVELOPING A COMMUNITY OUTREACH PROGRAM

INTRODUCTION

OVERVIEW OF CLARA'S PROFESSIONAL AND PERSONAL JOURNEY

Clara's life had been a journey of transformation, from a shy, overlooked girl to a confident and successful woman. She had harnessed her past experiences and used them to fuel her passion for helping others. Her unique ability to connect with her clients stemmed from the empathy and understanding born out of her own struggles. Clara's story is a powerful testament to resilience, growth, and the transformative power of embracing one's true self.

COMBINING PROFESSIONAL KNOWLEDGE WITH PERSONAL EXPERIENCES

Clara Used Her Own Life Experiences to Inform Her Therapeutic Practice

Clara's past was a tapestry of challenges and triumphs that she wove into her professional life. Her early feelings of isolation and misunderstanding gave her a deep well of empathy from which to draw. She knew firsthand what it felt like to be marginalized and misunderstood, and this enabled her to connect with her clients on a profound level.

In her therapy sessions, Clara often shared parts of her own journey, not to shift the focus onto herself, but to illustrate that change and healing were possible. Her clients found comfort in knowing that their therapist had walked a similar path and had come out stronger on the other side. Clara's ability to relate personally to their struggles created a safe space for her clients to open up and trust her with their vulnerabilities.

Her Past, Once a Source of Pain, Became a Wellspring of Strength and Wisdom

The incidents that once brought Clara pain had become the very source of her strength and wisdom.

She had learned to look at her past not as a series of unfortunate events but as experiences that had shaped her into the person she was today. This perspective shift allowed her to see the value in her hardships and use them to help others find their way.

Clara's personal growth was evident in her approach to therapy. She encouraged her clients to explore their own histories, to find meaning in their experiences, and to use those insights to build a better future. Her methods were a blend of professional techniques and personal insight, making her a uniquely effective therapist.

TRANSFORMATION FROM PAIN TO STRENGTH

Clara's Growth from a Young Girl Overshadowed by Her Brothers to a Confident Woman Who Found Her Path

Clara's childhood was marked by the constant feeling of being overshadowed by her popular brothers, Max and Ash. She often felt invisible and unimportant, which led to a period of intense self-doubt and isolation. However, these experiences also ignited a fire within her to carve out her own identity and path.

Her journey was not an easy one. Clara had to navigate through emotional turmoil, but each step she took brought her closer to understanding herself. Through therapy, education, and self-reflection, she began to see her worth and potential. This journey of self-discovery transformed her from a girl who felt overshadowed into a woman who stood confidently in her own light.

The Journey of Overcoming Feelings of Isolation and Finding Her Own Identity

Clara's path to self-discovery involved confronting the feelings of isolation that had plagued her during her youth. She realized that to truly overcome these feelings, she had to face them head-on. With the support of her friends, family, and Alexander, she started to explore her passions and interests, which eventually led her to psychology and writing.

Finding her identity was a gradual process. Clara delved into her studies with determination, finding solace and purpose in learning about human behavior and mental health. Her writing became an outlet for her emotions, a way to process her thoughts, and a means to reach out to others who might be feeling the same way she once did.

FLOURISHING RELATIONSHIP WITH ALEXANDER AND THEIR LOVING FAMILY

Clara and Alexander's Relationship Thrived, Built on Mutual Respect, Love, and Support

Clara's relationship with Alexander was a cornerstone of her personal journey. They met during a tumultuous time in her life, and his unwavering support helped her navigate through her darkest moments. Their relationship was built on a foundation of mutual respect, love, and support, which only strengthened over time.

Alexander admired Clara's resilience and her commitment to helping others. He was her biggest cheerleader, always encouraging her to pursue her dreams and passions. In return, Clara supported Alexander in his endeavors, creating a partnership that was balanced and nurturing.

Together, They Created a Loving and Nurturing Environment for Their Children, Fostering Strong Family Bonds

Clara and Alexander's love extended to their children, creating a home filled with warmth and affection. They made a conscious effort to foster strong family bonds, ensuring that their children, Eric, Ginny, and

Georgia, grew up in an environment where they felt loved and valued.

Family time was sacred in their household. They engaged in activities that brought them closer, from weekend adventures to quiet evenings spent reading or playing games. Clara and Alexander made sure to instill values of empathy, kindness, and resilience in their children, teaching them the importance of supporting one another and facing challenges together.

TESTAMENT TO RESILIENCE AND SELF-ACCEPTANCE

Clara's Journey is a Testament to Her Resilience, Demonstrating How Embracing One's True Self Can Lead to Fulfillment and Happiness

Clara's life story is a powerful testament to resilience and the importance of self-acceptance. She faced numerous challenges, but each one taught her valuable lessons and contributed to her growth. By embracing her true self, Clara found fulfillment and happiness that she once thought was unattainable.

Her resilience was evident in her ability to turn her pain into a source of strength. Clara's journey showed that it is possible to overcome adversity and emerge stronger. Her story is an inspiration to others, demonstrating that embracing one's true self can lead to a life filled with purpose and joy.

Reflection

Clara's professional and personal journey, marked by her resilience and self-acceptance, showcases the transformative power of combining personal experiences with professional knowledge. Her ability to connect with clients and help them heal, her flourishing relationship with Alexander, and the loving environment they created for their children are testaments to her strength and growth. Clara's story is an inspiring reminder that embracing one's true self and facing challenges head-on can lead to a life of fulfillment and happiness.

CHAPTER 1

CLARA'S INVITATION TO THE PSYCHOLOGY CONFERENCE

CLARA'S EXCITEMENT AND PREPARATION FOR THE MAJOR PSYCHOLOGY CONFERENCE

Clara was ecstatic when she received the invitation to speak at the prestigious National Psychology Conference. This was not just any conference; it was a gathering of some of the most respected minds in the field of psychology, and it provided a unique opportunity for Clara to share her journey and insights with a broader audience. The invitation was a testament to her hard work and dedication, and it felt like a validation of all the efforts she had put into her career.

OPPORTUNITY TO SHARE HER JOURNEY AND INSIGHTS WITH A BROADER AUDIENCE

The conference offered Clara a platform to discuss her unique approach to therapy, which blended professional knowledge with personal experience. Clara's therapy sessions were known for their warmth and empathy, qualities that stemmed from her own experiences of pain and healing. She had always believed that understanding and connecting with clients on a personal level was crucial for effective therapy, and this conference was her chance to explain why.

As she prepared her presentation, Clara reflected on her journey. She thought about her early years, feeling isolated and overshadowed by her brothers, and how those experiences had shaped her desire to help others. Her presentation would include personal anecdotes that illustrated the importance of empathy and resilience. She wanted to convey that her methods were not just based on textbooks but also on real-life experiences that had taught her valuable lessons about human nature and healing.

IMPORTANCE OF THE CONFERENCE IN CLARA'S CAREER

This conference was a significant milestone in Clara's career. Speaking at such a high-profile event would highlight her achievements and cement her reputation in the field of psychology. It was a chance to showcase her innovative approaches and to contribute to the ongoing discussions about best practices in therapy, particularly for adolescents.

Clara understood the importance of this opportunity. She spent weeks meticulously preparing her presentation, ensuring that it was both informative and engaging. She rehearsed her speech multiple times, refining her delivery to make sure it would resonate with the audience. She included case studies and data to support her points, as well as personal stories to illustrate the impact of her methods.

As the day of the conference approached, Clara felt a mix of excitement and nervousness. She knew that this was a pivotal moment in her career, one that could open doors to new opportunities and collaborations. She was eager to share her insights and to learn from other experts in the field.

On the day of the conference, Clara arrived early to familiarize herself with the venue and to calm her nerves. The room where she would be speaking was large, filled with rows of chairs that would soon be occupied by her peers and mentors. As she set up her presentation, she took a moment to reflect on how far she had come. From a young girl struggling with self-doubt and isolation, she had grown into a confident and respected professional.

When it was time for her to speak, Clara stepped up to the podium, her heart pounding with anticipation. She began her presentation by sharing her personal story, describing how her own experiences had influenced her decision to become a therapist. She spoke about the challenges she had faced and how they had shaped her approach to therapy.

Clara's presentation was well-received. The audience was captivated by her honesty and the depth of her insights. Many attendees approached her afterward to express their admiration and to discuss potential collaborations. One of those attendees was Dr. James Hart, a renowned psychologist specializing in family therapy.

Dr. Hart was particularly impressed with Clara's emphasis on empathy and personal connection. He believed that these qualities were often overlooked in traditional therapy practices, and he was eager to learn more about Clara's methods. They struck up a conversation, and by the end of the conference, they had agreed to collaborate on a community outreach program aimed at helping families rebuild trust and communication.

For Clara, the conference was a resounding success. It not only highlighted her achievements but also provided her with new opportunities to expand her impact. She left the conference feeling inspired and energized, ready to take on new challenges and to continue her journey of helping others heal and grow.

Reflection

Chapter 1 sets the stage for Clara's next phase in her professional life. The invitation to speak at the National Psychology Conference is a significant milestone that underscores her achievements and dedication to her field. The chapter highlights Clara's excitement and meticulous preparation for the conference, her impactful presentation that blends personal experience with professional knowledge, and the new opportunities that arise from this pivotal moment in her career. The conference serves as a testament to Clara's resilience and the transformative power of embracing one's true self, setting the tone for the rest of her journey.

CHAPTER 2

CLARA'S CONFERENCE SPEECH

CLARA'S OPENING REMARKS ABOUT HER CHILDHOOD AND FEELINGS OF ISOLATION

Clara stood at the podium, her heart pounding with a mix of excitement and nervousness. The room was filled with fellow psychologists, students, and professionals eager to hear her story. She took a deep breath, adjusted the microphone, and began her speech.

"Good morning, everyone. Thank you for being here today. I want to start by sharing a bit about my journey, as it has been instrumental in shaping my approach to therapy and my passion for helping adolescents."

EXPERIENCE OF FEELING ALONE AND MISUNDERSTOOD

Clara continued, "Growing up, I often felt alone and misunderstood. My brothers, Max and Ash, were very popular, always surrounded by friends and admirers. They were outgoing, athletic, and seemed to have everything figured out. In contrast, I was shy and introverted, often feeling like I was living in their shadow."

As she spoke, Clara could see heads nodding in the audience, indicating that many could relate to her feelings of isolation. "There were times when I felt invisible, as if my presence didn't matter. This sense of loneliness and misunderstanding was a heavy burden for a young girl to carry."

BROTHERS' POPULARITY AND HER FEELINGS OF EXCLUSION

Clara described the emotional impact of her brothers' popularity. "Max and Ash were the stars of our school. They excelled in sports, had a wide circle of friends, and were always the center of attention at social gatherings. Meanwhile, I struggled to find my place. I longed for the same acceptance and recognition they received, but it always seemed just out of reach."

She paused, letting her words sink in. "Feeling excluded and overlooked took a toll on my self-esteem. I began to believe that I wasn't good enough, that there was something inherently wrong with me. These feelings of inadequacy and exclusion shaped much of my early life."

THE PIVOTAL INCIDENT OF THE BABY BLANKET REVELATION

Clara recounted a particularly painful memory. "One of the most pivotal moments for me was at my brothers' birthday party. They thought it would be funny to reveal my baby blanket to everyone, something I had kept for comfort. It was meant to be a harmless joke, but for me, it was deeply humiliating."

She paused, recalling the sting of that day. "The laughter and teasing from their friends were too much to bear. I felt utterly exposed and humiliated. This incident led me to withdraw even further into myself."

Emotional Impact and Subsequent Withdrawal

"The humiliation I felt that day was overwhelming," Clara continued. "I started dressing in black, hoping to blend into the background. I avoided social interactions, convinced that people would only see me as the girl with the baby blanket. This period of my life was incredibly isolating."

She glanced around the room, seeing the empathy in the faces of her listeners. "I struggled with feelings of shame and worthlessness. It was a dark time, but it was also a turning point."

FINDING SOLACE IN STUDIES, FRIENDS, AND ALEXANDER

Clara then spoke about the turning point in her journey. "During this difficult time, I found solace in my studies. Books became my refuge, and I immersed myself in learning. It was through my studies that I began to regain a sense of purpose and direction."

"Another source of support came from my close friends and my boyfriend, Alexander," Clara continued, her voice softening as she mentioned his name. "Alexander was a constant presence, offering me unwavering support and understanding. My friends, too, stood by me, helping me navigate through the rough patches."

Support Systems That Helped Her Through Difficult Times

"The role of these support systems cannot be overstated," Clara emphasized. "My friends and Alexander provided a sense of belonging and acceptance that I had been missing. They reminded me that I was valued and loved, just as I was. This support was crucial in helping me rebuild my self-esteem and confidence."

DECISION TO STUDY PSYCHOLOGY AND BECOME A THERAPIST

Clara shared the motivations behind her career choice. "It was during this period of self-discovery that I decided to study psychology. I wanted to understand human behavior, not just to make sense of my own experiences, but also to help others who might be feeling the same way."

Desire to Understand Human Behavior and Help Others

"My desire to understand human behavior and help others became the driving force behind my career," Clara explained. "I found fulfillment in learning about the complexities of the human mind and the ways we can support one another through life's challenges."

Writing as a Therapeutic Outlet and a Means to Share Her Story

Clara also spoke about her passion for writing. "Writing became a therapeutic outlet for me. It allowed me to process my experiences and emotions in a way that was both healing and empowering. Through my writing, I was able to share my story and let others know that they were not alone in their struggles."

She concluded her speech with a message of hope and resilience. "My journey has taught me the importance of empathy, support, and resilience. It has shown me that we all have the strength within us to overcome adversity and find our own paths to fulfillment and happiness."

As Clara finished her speech, the room erupted in applause. She could see tears in the eyes of some audience members, while others wore expressions of deep contemplation. Her story had resonated with them, touching their hearts and minds in a profound way.

Reflection

Chapter 2 delves into Clara's powerful and moving speech at the National Psychology Conference. Through her candid recounting of her childhood experiences and the pivotal moments that shaped her, Clara connects deeply with her audience, highlighting the transformative power of empathy, support, and resilience. Her speech not only showcases her personal journey but also underscores the motivations behind her career as a therapist and writer, inspiring others to find strength in their own stories.

CHAPTER 3

AUDIENCE REACTION AND POST-SPEECH EVENTS

POSITIVE RECEPTION AND RESONANCE OF CLARA'S STORY WITH THE AUDIENCE

As Clara concluded her speech and stepped away from the podium, the room erupted in applause. The audience's response was overwhelming, with many standing in appreciation of her candid and heartfelt presentation. Clara could see the impact her story had made; some attendees had tears in their eyes, while others wore expressions of deep thought and empathy. The resonance of her story was palpable, and Clara felt a surge of gratitude for the opportunity to share her journey.

During the question-and-answer session that followed, numerous hands shot up. Attendees asked

Clara about her therapeutic techniques, her personal healing process, and how she balanced her professional and personal life. Clara answered each question thoughtfully, providing insights that further endeared her to the audience. Her vulnerability and authenticity struck a chord, making her not just a speaker but a beacon of hope and resilience for many.

MEETING DR. JAMES HART, A RENOWNED PSYCHOLOGIST

After the session ended, Clara was approached by many attendees who wanted to thank her personally and share their own stories of struggle and perseverance. Among the crowd was Dr. James Hart, a renowned psychologist known for his work in family therapy. Clara recognized him immediately; his books and articles had been a part of her own education and professional development.

His Admiration for Her Work and Story

Dr. Hart introduced himself and expressed his admiration for Clara's work and her inspiring story. "Clara, your speech was incredibly moving. Your ability to blend personal experience with professional insight is truly remarkable," he said. "I've been following your work for some time now, and seeing you speak today has only deepened my respect for you."

Clara was humbled by his words, knowing the weight that such praise carried coming from a figure like Dr. Hart. "Thank you, Dr. Hart. It means a lot coming from you. Your work has been an inspiration to me as well," she replied.

Conversation About Their Shared Goals and Interests

Their conversation quickly turned to their shared goals and interests. Dr. Hart was particularly interested in Clara's focus on empathy and personal connection in therapy. He shared his own experiences and the evolution of his approach to family therapy, emphasizing the importance of rebuilding trust and communication within families.

"One of the areas I've been focusing on is how we can support families in crisis," Dr. Hart explained. "Your approach to therapy, especially with adolescents, seems to align perfectly with some of the initiatives I'm working on. I think there's a lot we could do together."

Clara felt a surge of excitement. Collaborating with Dr. Hart was an opportunity she hadn't anticipated but one that felt incredibly promising. "I've always believed in the power of family support systems," Clara said. "It's an area I'm passionate about, especially given my own experiences. I'd love to explore how we can work together to make a difference."

Decision to Collaborate on a Community Outreach Program

Their discussion led to the idea of a community outreach program focused on rebuilding family trust and communication. Dr. Hart shared his vision of a program that offered workshops, support groups, and counseling sessions aimed at helping families heal and strengthen their bonds.

Clara was immediately on board. "This is exactly the kind of initiative I've been hoping to be a part of," she said. "There's so much we can do to help families understand each other better and build healthier relationships."

By the end of their conversation, they had decided to collaborate on the project. Dr. Hart would bring his extensive experience and established network, while Clara would contribute her unique approach and insights, particularly her work with adolescents. They planned to start the program in Clara's hometown, a place filled with memories of her own family's challenges and triumphs.

Post-Speech Events: Planning and Implementation

In the weeks following the conference, Clara and Dr. Hart worked tirelessly to bring their vision to life. They held numerous planning sessions, outlining the structure and goals of the outreach program. They designed workshops tailored to address common family issues, such as communication barriers, trust rebuilding, and emotional support.

Clara reached out to her network of colleagues and friends in her hometown, gathering a team of dedicated professionals who shared their vision. They secured funding from local organizations and applied for grants to support their efforts. The community was enthusiastic about the initiative, eager to see the positive changes it could bring.

Launch of the Community Outreach Program

The launch event for the community outreach program was a significant milestone. Clara and Dr. Hart stood before a crowd of local families, educators, and community leaders, sharing their vision and the resources they had developed. The program included interactive workshops, counseling sessions, and support groups, all aimed at fostering understanding and healing within families.

Clara felt a deep sense of fulfillment as she watched the program come to life. Seeing families engage in open dialogue, participate in activities designed to build trust, and support each other was incredibly rewarding. The positive feedback they received affirmed that they were on the right path.

Impact on the Community

The impact of the community outreach program was profound. Families reported improved communication and stronger relationships. Parents and children alike expressed gratitude for the tools and support they had received. Clara and Dr. Hart's collaboration had not only brought tangible benefits to individual families but had also fostered a sense of community and mutual support.

Through this initiative, Clara was able to help not just individual clients but entire families. She saw the impact of her work in the smiles and gratitude of the people she helped. It was incredibly fulfilling to know that she was making a significant difference in her community. Her experiences reaffirmed her belief in the importance of healing, forgiveness, and resilience. Clara's journey from the shadows to a position of strength and fulfillment continued to inspire those around her, proving that with empathy and dedication, one can overcome any adversity.

CHAPTER 4

RETURNING TO HER HOMETOWN

CLARA'S RETURN TO HER HOMETOWN FOR THE COMMUNITY OUTREACH PROGRAM

Returning to her hometown was a significant step for Clara. It was a place filled with memories of both pain and growth, a backdrop to her journey from a struggling adolescent to a successful therapist and writer. Launching the community outreach program there was both a professional milestone and a personal reconciliation with her past.

As the car wound its way through familiar streets, Clara felt a surge of emotions. She passed by her old school, the park where she used to play, and the neighborhoods that held so many memories. Each landmark triggered a flood of recollections, some joyful and some painful. This return was not just about launching a program; it was about acknowledging and embracing her past.

MIXED EMOTIONS OF REVISITING A PLACE OF PAIN AND GROWTH

Clara experienced a mix of emotions as she revisited her hometown. The sight of familiar places brought back memories of her struggles, the feeling of being overshadowed by her brothers, and the pain of feeling misunderstood and isolated. But alongside these memories were the recollections of her journey of growth, the friendships she had formed, and the support systems that had helped her find her way.

Walking down the streets, she remembered the shy girl she once was, the girl who hid behind black clothes and avoided social interactions. She also remembered the pivotal moments that had sparked her transformation, like the encouragement from her friends and the unconditional support from Alexander. The town held a mirror to her past, reflecting both the pain she had endured and the strength she had developed.

RECONNECTING WITH OLD FRIENDS AND MENTORS

One of the most rewarding aspects of returning home was reconnecting with old friends and mentors who had played significant roles in her journey. Clara arranged to meet with Amy, Alex, and Mia, her close friends from high school. They had been her pillars of support during her toughest times, and their bond had remained strong over the years.

Their reunion was filled with laughter and reminiscing. They visited their old hangouts, sharing stories and catching up on each other's lives. Amy had become a successful photographer, Alex was a respected painter, and Mia had published several novels. Seeing how they had all thrived brought a sense of pride and fulfillment to Clara.

Clara also made time to visit her old high school. Walking through the halls, she was flooded with memories of her teenage years. She met with several of her former teachers, who had always encouraged her to pursue her interests and believe in herself. One of these teachers was Mrs. Thompson, her art teacher, who had been a constant source of inspiration and support.

Visits to Her Old High School and Meetings with Former Teachers

Mrs. Thompson greeted Clara with a warm hug. "Clara, it's so wonderful to see you! I've heard about all the amazing work you've been doing. I always knew you had a special gift."

Clara smiled, feeling a wave of gratitude. "Thank you, Mrs. Thompson. Your support meant the world to me. I wouldn't be where I am today without your encouragement."

They walked through the art room, now filled with new students' work, but still carrying the same creative energy. Clara shared her plans for the community outreach program, and Mrs. Thompson expressed her excitement and offered her full support. It was a full-circle moment for Clara, standing in the place where her passion for art and helping others had first been nurtured.

Reflections on Her Past and the Support She Received

Reflecting on her past, Clara realized how much the support she had received had shaped her journey. Her friends, teachers, and Alexander had all played crucial roles in helping her navigate her challenges and find her path. Their belief in her had given her the strength to believe in herself.

Clara thought about the times when she had felt completely lost, and how these people had guided her back to herself. Their kindness and support had been lifelines, pulling her through the darkest moments. She understood now more than ever the importance of having a strong support system, and this realization fueled her determination to make the community outreach program a success.

The program aimed to provide the same kind of support and guidance to others, helping families rebuild trust and communication. Clara wanted to create a space where people could find understanding and encouragement, just as she had found in her mentors and friends. She believed that by fostering these connections, the program could help individuals and families heal and grow.

As Clara prepared for the program's launch, she felt a deep sense of fulfillment. She was not just returning to her hometown; she was coming back as a symbol of hope and resilience. Her journey from pain to strength, from isolation to connection, was a testament to the transformative power of empathy and support.

Reflection

Chapter 4 captures the emotional and reflective experience of Clara returning to her hometown. It highlights the mixed emotions of revisiting a place filled with memories of pain and growth, the joy of reconnecting with old friends and mentors, and the powerful reflections on the support that had shaped her journey. Through these experiences, Clara reaffirms her commitment to helping others find their path to healing and growth, setting the stage for the impactful work of the community outreach program.

CHAPTER 5

DEVELOPING THE COMMUNITY OUTREACH PROGRAM

CLARA AND DR. HART'S COLLABORATIVE EFFORTS

Clara and Dr. James Hart dove into their collaboration with a shared vision and enthusiasm. Both were passionate about creating a program that would address the deep-rooted issues within families and help them heal. They spent countless hours brainstorming, planning, and refining their ideas to develop a comprehensive community outreach program that would truly make a difference.

DESIGNING PROGRAMS TO HELP FAMILIES COMMUNICATE AND HEAL

Clara and Dr. Hart started by identifying the key issues that families in their community faced. They conducted surveys and held focus groups to understand the unique challenges and needs of these families. Their findings highlighted common problems such as lack of communication, unresolved conflicts, and a general sense of disconnection.

To address these issues, Clara and Dr. Hart designed a series of workshops, support groups, and family counseling sessions aimed at fostering understanding and forgiveness. They wanted to create safe spaces where families could openly discuss their problems and work towards solutions together.

ORGANIZING WORKSHOPS, SUPPORT GROUPS, AND FAMILY COUNSELING SESSIONS

The workshops were carefully crafted to cover a range of topics relevant to family dynamics. They included sessions on effective communication, conflict resolution, building trust, and fostering emotional intimacy. Each workshop was interactive, encouraging participants to actively engage and practice the skills they were learning.

Support groups were another critical component of the program. These groups provided a platform for individuals to share their experiences and receive support from others facing similar challenges. Clara and Dr. Hart facilitated these groups, ensuring a respectful and empathetic environment where participants could express themselves freely.

Family counseling sessions were tailored to the specific needs of each family. Clara and Dr. Hart conducted these sessions together, combining their expertise to offer comprehensive guidance. They used various therapeutic techniques to help families address their issues, heal old wounds, and rebuild their relationships.

Specific Activities Designed to Address Various Aspects of Family Dynamics and Promote Healing

One of the workshops focused on "Effective Communication Skills." In this session, participants learned about active listening, expressing emotions constructively, and using "I" statements to communicate their needs without blaming others. Role-playing exercises allowed families to practice these skills in a supportive setting.

Another workshop, "Building Trust and Emotional Intimacy," aimed to help families reconnect on a deeper level. Activities included trust-building exercises and guided discussions about vulnerability and empathy. Families were encouraged to share their feelings and experiences, fostering a sense of closeness and mutual understanding.

The support groups featured themed discussions, such as "Parenting Challenges" and "Navigating Teen Issues." These groups provided a space for parents and teens to discuss their concerns, share advice, and offer emotional support. Clara and Dr. Hart guided these discussions, ensuring that they remained constructive and focused.

Family counseling sessions often involved activities like "Family Mapping," where families created visual representations of their relationships and dynamics. This activity helped them identify patterns and areas that needed improvement. Clara and Dr. Hart used these maps to guide their counseling sessions, helping families develop strategies to enhance their interactions and resolve conflicts.

IMPACT OF THE PROGRAMS ON THE COMMUNITY

The community outreach program quickly gained traction and became a beacon of hope for many families. Word spread about the positive changes participants were experiencing, and more families signed up to take part in the workshops, support groups, and counseling sessions.

Positive Changes in Family Dynamics

The impact of the program on family dynamics was profound. Many families reported significant improvements in their relationships. Parents who had struggled to communicate with their children found new ways to connect and understand each other. Siblings who had been distant began to rebuild their bonds, and couples learned to resolve conflicts more effectively.

One family, the Thompsons, shared their story with Clara and Dr. Hart. Before joining the program, they had been on the verge of breaking apart. Communication had broken down, and resentment had built up over the years. Through the workshops and counseling sessions, they learned to listen to each other and express their feelings without judgment. Over time, they healed old wounds and strengthened their relationships, emerging as a more united and supportive family.

Personal Stories of Healing and Gratitude

Clara and Dr. Hart were deeply moved by the personal stories of healing and gratitude they heard from participants. One evening, after a particularly powerful support group session, a mother approached Clara with tears in her eyes. "Thank you," she said. "This program has saved my family. We were drifting apart, and I didn't know how to bring us back together. You've given us the tools to heal and grow closer."

Another participant, a teenage boy named Jason, shared his experience during a family counseling session. "I used to feel like my parents didn't understand me at all," he admitted. "But now, I feel like they actually listen to me. We're getting along so much better, and I feel more supported than ever."

These stories reinforced the importance of the work Clara and Dr. Hart were doing. They saw firsthand how the program was transforming lives, bringing families closer together, and fostering a sense of community and mutual support.

Reflection

Chapter 5 details the development and impact of the community outreach program designed by Clara and Dr. Hart. Their collaborative efforts led to the creation of workshops, support groups, and family counseling sessions that addressed critical issues within families. The program's success was evident in the positive changes in family dynamics and the personal stories of healing and gratitude from participants. Clara's commitment to helping others heal and grow continued to inspire those around her, demonstrating the transformative power of empathy, support, and resilience.

CHAPTER 6

CLARA'S CONTINUED IMPACT AND FULFILLMENT

THE FULFILLMENT CLARA FINDS IN HELPING OTHERS

Clara's journey had always been driven by a desire to help others, and her work in the community outreach program solidified this passion. Each day, she saw firsthand the impact of her efforts, and it filled her with immense fulfillment. Knowing that she was making a positive difference in people's lives was a source of profound satisfaction for Clara. She found joy in the small victories: a breakthrough in a counseling session, a heartfelt thank you from a participant, or a family expressing newfound hope and unity.

PERSONAL SATISFACTION FROM SEEING THE POSITIVE EFFECTS OF HER WORK

The positive effects of Clara's work were evident in the transformations she witnessed. Families that had been on the brink of breaking apart found new ways to connect and support each other. Children who had felt misunderstood and neglected began to open up and trust their parents. Couples who had been locked in a cycle of conflict learned to communicate and resolve their differences. Each success story brought Clara a deep sense of satisfaction and purpose. She often reflected on how far she had come from her own struggles, and how those experiences now enabled her to guide others towards healing.

One particular family, the Johnsons, stood out to Clara. They had joined the program with severe communication issues and a sense of hopelessness. Through the workshops and counseling sessions, they learned to listen to each other and express their feelings constructively. Clara watched as their interactions transformed from tense and confrontational to open and supportive. When they completed the program, they wrote Clara a letter of gratitude, describing the positive changes they had experienced. This reaffirmed Clara's belief in the power of her work and filled her with a deep sense of accomplishment.

REAFFIRMATION OF HER BELIEFS IN HEALING, FORGIVENESS, AND RESILIENCE

Clara's experiences in the community outreach program reaffirmed her core beliefs in healing, forgiveness, and resilience. She had always believed that no matter how deep the wounds, it was possible to heal with the right support and tools. The program provided a space for families to address their issues, forgive each other, and move forward stronger than before. Clara saw resilience in the faces of the participants, in their willingness to confront their problems and work towards a better future. Each story of healing and growth reinforced her conviction that resilience was at the heart of the human spirit.

One of the most poignant moments for Clara was when a young girl named Emily, who had been struggling with feelings of abandonment after her parents' divorce, found the courage to share her emotions during a support group session. Clara watched as Emily's mother, who had been unaware of the depth of her daughter's pain, listened with tears in her eyes. Through the guidance of the program, they began to rebuild their relationship. This experience highlighted the importance of creating opportunities for open communication and forgiveness, and it reaffirmed Clara's belief in the transformative power of empathy and support.

CLARA'S JOURNEY INSPIRING OTHERS IN THE COMMUNITY

Clara's journey from a place of pain and isolation to one of strength and fulfillment continued to inspire others in the community. Her story resonated with many, showing them that it was possible to overcome adversity and find purpose and joy. Clara often shared her personal experiences in her workshops and counseling sessions, using her own life as an example of resilience and transformation. Her honesty and vulnerability made her a relatable figure, and many participants found hope and encouragement in her journey.

Clara became a sought-after speaker in the community, invited to schools, community centers, and local events to share her story and insights. Each time she spoke, she saw the impact her words had on her audience. People approached her afterward, thanking her for her openness and sharing their own stories of struggle and triumph. Clara's journey not only inspired individuals but also fostered a sense of collective strength and support within the community.

DEMONSTRATING THE TRANSFORMATIVE POWER OF EMPATHY AND DEDICATION

Through her work, Clara demonstrated the transformative power of empathy and dedication in helping others heal and grow. She approached each family, each individual, with genuine compassion and a commitment to their well-being. Clara believed that empathy was the key to building trust and creating a safe space for healing. Her dedication to her work was evident in the long hours she spent planning workshops, leading sessions, and providing one-on-one support. She was driven by a deep-seated belief in the potential for positive change.

Clara's approach was holistic, addressing not just the immediate issues but also the underlying emotional and psychological needs of the families she worked with. She used a combination of therapeutic techniques, personal insights, and practical strategies to guide them towards healing. Her dedication extended beyond the formal sessions; she often followed up with participants, checking in on their progress and offering additional support as needed.

The impact of Clara's empathy and dedication was reflected in the lasting changes she saw in the community. Families who had once been fractured found new strength and unity. Individuals who had felt lost and unsupported discovered their own resilience and ability to thrive. Clara's work created ripples of positive change, fostering a culture of empathy, support, and growth.

Reflection

Chapter 6 highlights the profound fulfillment Clara finds in her work, the personal satisfaction of seeing the positive effects of her efforts, and the reaffirmation of her beliefs in healing, forgiveness, and resilience. Clara's journey continues to inspire others in the community, demonstrating the transformative power of empathy and dedication. Her story is a testament to the impact one person can make when driven by compassion and a commitment to helping others heal and grow. Clara's ongoing journey of fulfillment and impact underscores the enduring themes of resilience, empathy, and the power of personal transformation.

CHAPTER 7

REFLECTION ON CLARA'S JOURNEY

SUMMARY OF CLARA'S ACHIEVEMENTS AND HER ONGOING JOURNEY

Clara's achievements are a testament to her resilience, perseverance, and unwavering dedication to personal and professional growth. From her early struggles with feelings of isolation and inadequacy to her transformation into a confident and impactful therapist, Clara's journey has been nothing short of extraordinary. She has not only excelled in her field, earning respect and recognition for her innovative approaches to therapy, but she has also made significant contributions to her community through her outreach programs. Clara's ongoing journey of growth and fulfillment continues to inspire those around her, demonstrating that with determination and self-belief, one can overcome any obstacle.

BALANCE OF PROFESSIONAL SUCCESS AND FAMILY LIFE

One of Clara's most remarkable achievements is her ability to balance her professional success with her roles as a mother and wife. Despite the demands of her career, Clara has always prioritized her family, ensuring that she is present and engaged in their lives. She and Alexander have created a loving and supportive environment for their children, Eric, Ginny, and Georgia, instilling in them the values of empathy, resilience, and dedication. Clara's ability to juggle her professional and personal responsibilities is a testament to her exceptional time management skills and her deep commitment to both her career and her family. Her life is a harmonious blend of professional fulfillment and personal happiness, showing that it is possible to achieve success in both realms.

Her Lasting Impact on the Community and the People She Helps

Clara's impact on her community and the people she helps is profound and lasting. Through her work as a therapist and her involvement in the community outreach program, Clara has touched countless lives. Families have found healing and strength, individuals have discovered their own resilience, and the community as a whole has become more connected and supportive. Clara's dedication to fostering understanding, empathy, and communication within families has brought about positive changes that will resonate for generations. The gratitude and admiration expressed by those she has helped are a testament to the significant and enduring impact of her work.

Clara's Story as a Testament to the Power of Healing and Personal Growth

Clara's story is a powerful testament to the transformative power of healing and personal growth. Her journey from a place of pain and isolation to one of strength and fulfillment illustrates the potential for positive change that exists within each of us. Clara's ability to turn her struggles into sources of strength and wisdom is a reminder that our past does not define us; rather, it shapes us and gives us the tools we need to build a better future. Her story underscores the importance of embracing one's true self, seeking out supportive relationships, and dedicating oneself to continuous growth and self-improvement.

ENCOURAGEMENT TO EMBRACE ONE'S TRUE SELF AND FIND STRENGTH IN VULNERABILITY AND LOVE

Clara's journey encourages others to embrace their true selves and find strength in vulnerability and love. She has shown that it is through acknowledging and accepting our vulnerabilities that we can truly grow and heal. Clara's life is a testament to the power of love—love for oneself, love for others, and the love and support of family and friends. Her story inspires others to be authentic, to seek out connections that nurture and support them, and to believe in their own potential for growth and happiness. Clara's message is clear: by embracing our true selves and finding strength in our vulnerabilities, we can overcome any challenge and achieve a life filled with fulfillment and joy.

Conclusion

In conclusion, Clara's journey is a beacon of hope and resilience. Her achievements in both her professional and personal life, her lasting impact on her community, and her inspiring story of healing and personal growth serve as powerful reminders of what is possible when we embrace our true selves and dedicate ourselves to helping others. Clara's life is a testament to the transformative power of empathy, support, and love. As she continues her journey, she remains a source of inspiration and encouragement for all who seek to overcome adversity and find strength in vulnerability and love. Clara's story is a powerful reminder that with determination, resilience, and the support of loved ones, we can achieve anything we set our minds to and create lives filled with meaning, purpose, and joy.

PART FOUR
MAX AND ASH- A JOURNEY TO RESTAURANT SUCCESS

INTRODUCTION

INTRODUCTION TO MAX AND ASH'S CLOSE RELATIONSHIP AND FAMILY BACKGROUND

Max and Ash grew up in a household where love and support were abundant. Their parents, Charlotte and Asher, created a nurturing environment that emphasized the importance of family, hard work, and dedication. As the eldest of the twins, Max often took on the role of protector, while Ash was his constant companion. Their older sister, Clara, was an integral part of their lives, providing a balance to the brothers' dynamic.

Charlotte and Asher were role models for their children, demonstrating the value of persistence and the joy of achieving goals through hard work. Asher, a successful artist and businessman, and Charlotte, a dedicated homemaker, instilled in their children the belief that dreams could be realized with dedication and effort. They encouraged Max and Ash to explore their interests and supported them in every endeavor, fostering a sense of confidence and ambition in the boys.

EARLY LOVE FOR COOKING DURING FAMILY GATHERINGS

The brothers' love for cooking was kindled during the many family gatherings held at their home. These gatherings were always filled with laughter, story-telling, and, most importantly, food. Charlotte, an excellent cook herself, would prepare elaborate meals, and it wasn't long before Max and Ash wanted to join her in the kitchen.

Their initial attempts at cooking were simple – making sandwiches or helping to stir a pot – but as they grew older, their curiosity and enthusiasm led them to experiment with more complex recipes. They loved watching cooking shows and reading cookbooks, often trying to replicate the dishes they saw. The kitchen became their playground, a place where they could create and explore.

One memorable family gathering involved a friendly competition between Max and Ash to see who could make the best dessert. Max decided to bake a classic chocolate cake, while Ash, always the more adventurous, attempted a lemon tart. The family judged both dishes, and while Max's cake was a hit for its rich flavor, Ash's tart surprised everyone with its perfect balance of sweetness and tanginess. This competition not only showcased their budding skills but also highlighted their different approaches to cooking – Max's focus on perfecting traditional flavors and Ash's penchant for innovation.

DREAM OF OPENING THEIR OWN RESTAURANT

As they spent more time in the kitchen, the idea of opening their own restaurant began to take shape. It was during a late-night conversation after a particularly successful family dinner that they first articulated this dream. They envisioned a place where they could share their culinary creations with the world, a restaurant that would combine Max's culinary expertise with Ash's innovative ideas.

Their parents were supportive from the start, encouraging them to pursue their passion. Charlotte often told them, "If you love what you do, you'll never work a day in your life." This advice resonated deeply with Max and Ash, strengthening their resolve to turn their dream into reality.

They started planning and dreaming in earnest. They sketched out ideas for their future restaurant, imagining the layout, the type of cuisine they would serve, and even the ambiance they wanted to create. Their shared dream became a common goal that brought them even closer together. They vowed to turn their passion for cooking and their bond as brothers into a successful culinary venture, one that would not only showcase their talents but also bring people together through the joy of good food.

This vision of owning a restaurant became a driving force in their lives, influencing their choices and guiding their paths as they moved from high school to higher education and eventually into their respective fields of culinary arts and business management. Their journey was just beginning, but the foundation was solid – built on love, family, and a shared dream of culinary excellence.

CHAPTER 1
PURSUING THEIR PASSION

MAX'S DECISION TO ATTEND CULINARY SCHOOL

Max's fascination with flavors and culinary techniques began at a young age. His curiosity led him to experiment with different ingredients, always seeking to create dishes that would delight and impress his family and friends. He spent hours watching cooking shows, reading culinary books, and practicing his skills in the family kitchen. Max's dedication and natural talent for cooking became apparent to everyone around him.

After high school, Max knew that he wanted to take his passion for cooking to the next level. He researched various culinary schools and decided to apply to one of the most prestigious institutions in the country, renowned for its rigorous training and esteemed faculty. The application process was competitive, but Max's impressive portfolio of self-taught skills and his genuine passion for cooking secured him a spot.

Attending culinary school was a transformative experience for Max. He was exposed to a wide range of culinary techniques and cuisines, from classic French cuisine to modern molecular gastronomy. The rigorous training pushed him to refine his skills and expand his culinary knowledge. Max thrived in this environment, absorbing everything he could from his instructors and peers.

One of Max's most influential mentors was Chef Pierre, a master of French cuisine known for his meticulous attention to detail and innovative approach to cooking. Chef Pierre recognized Max's potential and took him under his wing, offering personalized guidance and encouragement. Under Chef Pierre's mentorship, Max learned the importance of precision, creativity, and passion in every dish he created.

Max's dedication to his craft paid off as he consistently ranked at the top of his class. He participated in numerous culinary competitions, earning accolades and recognition for his innovative dishes. These experiences not only honed his skills but also boosted his confidence, solidifying his dream of becoming a renowned chef.

ASH'S CHOICE TO STUDY BUSINESS AND HOSPITALITY MANAGEMENT

While Max was perfecting his culinary skills, Ash was equally driven to pursue his passion, albeit in a different direction. Ash had always been intrigued by the operational side of running a restaurant. He understood that behind every successful restaurant was a well-oiled machine of management and customer service. Ash believed that mastering these aspects was crucial to turning their dream into a reality.

Ash decided to study business and hospitality management at a leading university. His coursework covered a broad spectrum of topics, including finance, marketing, human resources, and customer service. Ash's natural aptitude for leadership and organization made him a standout student. He was particularly drawn to courses on restaurant management, where he learned about the intricacies of running a successful dining establishment.

One of Ash's key mentors was Professor Davis, an experienced hospitality manager who had worked with some of the top restaurants in the country. Professor Davis emphasized the importance of creating a memorable dining experience, from the quality of the food to the ambiance of the restaurant and the efficiency of the service. Under his guidance, Ash developed a keen understanding of the various elements that contribute to a restaurant's success.

Ash also gained practical experience through internships at renowned restaurants. These internships provided him with a firsthand look at the daily operations of successful establishments. He worked in different roles, from front-of-house positions like host and server to back-of-house roles such as inventory management and supply chain coordination. This hands-on experience was invaluable, giving Ash a comprehensive understanding of what it takes to run a restaurant smoothly.

During his studies, Ash also focused on developing strong customer service skills. He understood that the way guests were treated could make or break a restaurant's reputation. Ash learned techniques for managing customer expectations, handling complaints gracefully, and creating a welcoming atmosphere that encouraged repeat business.

Max and Ash's Shared Vision

Despite their different educational paths, Max and Ash remained closely connected through their shared vision of opening a restaurant. They frequently discussed their ideas and plans, combining Max's culinary creativity with Ash's business acumen. Their complementary skills and mutual respect for each other's expertise laid the foundation for a strong partnership.

Max and Ash spent their weekends and holidays working together on their business plan. They researched market trends, studied successful restaurant models, and brainstormed innovative concepts that would set their restaurant apart. Their dream was to create a place where exceptional food and outstanding service came together to offer an unforgettable dining experience.

As they neared the completion of their studies, Max and Ash began scouting for potential locations for their restaurant. They wanted a place that was accessible, had a welcoming atmosphere, and could accommodate their vision. Their search eventually led them back to their hometown, where they found a charming spot that felt perfect for their dream project.

With their education complete and their vision clear, Max and Ash were ready to embark on the next chapter of their journey. They knew that the road ahead would be challenging, but they were prepared to face any obstacles with the same determination and dedication that had brought them this far. Their dream of opening a restaurant was no longer just a distant goal; it was becoming a reality, fueled by their passion and hard work.

CHAPTER 2

STARTING THEIR FIRST RESTAURANT: "SIBLING SAVORS"

FINDING A SMALL, COZY PLACE IN THEIR HOMETOWN

After completing their respective educations, Max and Ash returned to their hometown, a place filled with nostalgic memories and a supportive community that had watched them grow. They knew that starting their first restaurant here would not only be a nod to their roots but also provide them with a familiar environment where they could establish themselves.

They spent weeks searching for the perfect location, touring numerous sites, and weighing the pros and cons of each. Their criteria were specific: they wanted a place that exuded warmth and charm, somewhere intimate enough to create a personal dining experience but large enough to accommodate their ambitions.

One day, while walking through the quaint streets of their hometown, they stumbled upon an old bookstore that had recently closed down. The moment they stepped inside, they were captivated by its potential. The space was small but inviting, with wooden floors that creaked underfoot and large windows that let in plenty of natural light. It had an unassuming charm that matched their vision perfectly.

The brothers could immediately picture their restaurant there. They imagined diners sitting at rustic wooden tables, enjoying meals prepared with love and care. The cozy atmosphere was exactly what they wanted – a place where guests could feel at home while savoring exceptional food. After some negotiation, they secured the lease, and "Sibling Savors" was born.

NAMING THE RESTAURANT "SIBLING SAVORS"

Choosing the name "Sibling Savors" was a heartfelt decision that reflected their journey and bond. The name encapsulated their relationship as brothers and their shared passion for cooking. It was a tribute to the countless hours they had spent together in the kitchen, experimenting with recipes and dreaming about their future.

The name also conveyed a sense of togetherness and family, which was central to their vision for the restaurant. They wanted their guests to feel the same warmth and connection that had inspired them throughout their lives. "Sibling Savors" was not just a restaurant; it was an embodiment of their shared dream and a place where they could share their love for food with others.

ROLES AND RESPONSIBILITIES

With the location secured and the name decided, Max and Ash set about transforming the old bookstore into their dream restaurant. They divided their responsibilities based on their strengths and expertise, ensuring that every aspect of the restaurant was handled with care and precision.

Max as Head Chef

Max took on the role of head chef, dedicating himself to creating unique and delicious dishes that would set "Sibling Savors" apart. His education at culinary school had equipped him with a vast repertoire of techniques and knowledge, and he was eager to put it all into practice.

Max spent countless hours in the kitchen, experimenting with different ingredients and flavors. He crafted a menu that showcased his culinary creativity, blending traditional dishes with innovative twists. Each dish was a reflection of his passion for cooking and his commitment to excellence.

One of Max's signature dishes was a deconstructed shepherd's pie, which became an instant favorite among their patrons. He used the finest locally-sourced ingredients, ensuring that every bite was bursting with flavor. Max's attention to detail and dedication to perfection were evident in every dish that left the kitchen.

Ash Managing the Business Side

While Max focused on the culinary aspects, Ash took charge of the business operations. His background in business and hospitality management had prepared him well for the challenges ahead. He was responsible for everything from staff management to customer service, making sure that the restaurant ran smoothly and efficiently.

Ash meticulously handled the finances, keeping a close eye on expenses and revenues. He knew that maintaining a healthy balance sheet was crucial to their success, especially in the early stages. He also took care of marketing and promotions, using social media and local advertising to attract customers and build their brand.

One of Ash's key initiatives was to create a welcoming and inclusive atmosphere for both the staff and the guests. He believed that happy employees would lead to happy customers, so he invested time in training the staff, ensuring they understood the restaurant's ethos and values. Ash fostered a sense of camaraderie among the team, making "Sibling Savors" not just a workplace but a family.

Renovation and Preparation

Transforming the old bookstore into a restaurant was no small feat. Max and Ash rolled up their sleeves and got to work, involving themselves in every aspect of the renovation. They wanted to preserve the building's original charm while adding elements that would enhance the dining experience.

They chose a rustic yet elegant décor, with wooden tables and chairs, vintage light fixtures, and shelves lined with cookbooks and culinary memorabilia. The large windows were adorned with simple curtains, allowing natural light to flood the space during the day and creating a cozy ambiance at night.

The kitchen was outfitted with state-of-the-art equipment, ensuring that Max had everything he needed to create his culinary masterpieces. They also designed a small but functional bar area, where guests could enjoy a selection of wines and cocktails curated by Max and Ash themselves.

Grand Opening and Initial Reception

The grand opening of "Sibling Savors" was an event to remember. The brothers invited family, friends, and local community members to join them in celebrating the realization of their dream. Charlotte and Asher were there, beaming with pride, along with Clara, who had been a constant source of support.

The restaurant was packed, with guests eager to taste the creations of the talented brothers. Max and Ash worked tirelessly, ensuring that everything went smoothly. The food received rave reviews, and the warm, welcoming atmosphere made everyone feel at home.

The initial reception was overwhelmingly positive, and word of mouth quickly spread. Max and Ash knew that the journey ahead would be challenging, but the success of their opening night gave them the confidence and motivation to keep pushing forward.

Looking Ahead

With "Sibling Savors" up and running, Max and Ash were ready to face the challenges of the restaurant business head-on. They knew that maintaining high standards and continuously innovating were key to their long-term success. Their journey had just begun, and they were determined to make their mark in the culinary world, one delicious dish at a time.

CHAPTER 3

CHALLENGES AND EARLY STRUGGLES

COMPETITION WITH OTHER RESTAURANTS AND FINANCIAL MANAGEMENT

The initial phase of running "Sibling Savors" was fraught with challenges. The restaurant industry in their hometown was highly competitive, with several well-established eateries already enjoying loyal followings. Max and Ash knew that they had to offer something unique to attract customers away from these established venues. However, standing out in a crowded market was easier said than done.

Financial management was another significant hurdle. Despite their meticulous planning, unexpected expenses cropped up regularly. Equipment repairs, supply costs, and marketing efforts quickly added up, creating a constant strain on their budget. They had to be extremely careful with their spending, ensuring that every dollar was used wisely to support the restaurant's growth and sustainability.

They Faced Difficulties in Attracting Customers and Maintaining a Steady Cash Flow

Initially, attracting customers to "Sibling Savors" proved to be a daunting task. Max and Ash had invested heavily in creating a cozy, welcoming atmosphere and a menu filled with delicious, unique dishes, but convincing people to try their restaurant was challenging. They realized that without a steady stream of customers, maintaining cash flow and covering their expenses would be impossible.

They launched various marketing campaigns to draw in the crowd. They distributed flyers, offered special promotions, and engaged with potential customers on social media. Despite these efforts, progress was slow. There were days when the restaurant was nearly empty, and the brothers found themselves questioning their decisions and strategies.

FEELINGS OF BEING OVERWHELMED DURING SLOW BUSINESS PERIODS

During these slow business periods, Max and Ash often felt overwhelmed. The empty tables and mounting bills were a constant source of stress. There were nights when they stayed awake, worrying about how they would make ends meet and keep their dream alive. The pressure was immense, and the fear of failure loomed large.

Max, who poured his heart into every dish, sometimes felt disheartened when he saw the lack of customers. He began to doubt his culinary skills and whether his passion for cooking could translate into a successful business. Ash, responsible for the business side of things, felt the weight of financial responsibilities. He constantly recalculated budgets, looked for cost-saving measures, and brainstormed new marketing ideas.

COMMITMENT TO HARD WORK AND LONG HOURS

Despite these challenges, Max and Ash remained unwavering in their commitment to their dream. They knew that success would not come overnight and that they needed to persevere through the tough times. They resolved to work even harder, determined to turn their vision into reality.

Max Focused on Refining Recipes and Experimenting with New Dishes

Max immersed himself in his culinary work, continuously refining recipes and experimenting with new dishes. He believed that the quality of their food would ultimately set them apart from the competition. He spent countless hours in the kitchen, testing new ingredients, perfecting flavors, and creating innovative presentations. His dedication to excellence never wavered, and each dish was a testament to his passion for cooking.

Max also sought feedback from their initial customers, using their comments to improve the menu. He introduced seasonal specials, offered tasting menus, and even hosted cooking demonstrations to engage with the community and showcase his skills. His relentless pursuit of culinary perfection began to pay off as diners started to appreciate the unique flavors and meticulous preparation of his dishes.

Ash Handled the Logistical Aspects, from Ordering Supplies to Training Staff

While Max focused on the kitchen, Ash took charge of the logistical aspects of running the restaurant. He managed the supply chain, ensuring that they always had the freshest ingredients. He developed relationships with local suppliers, negotiating deals to keep costs manageable. Ash also focused on staff training, emphasizing the importance of excellent customer service and creating a welcoming atmosphere.

Ash introduced new systems to streamline operations, from inventory management to scheduling shifts. He organized regular staff meetings to address any issues and foster a sense of teamwork and shared purpose. His efforts to create a positive work environment were essential in maintaining high morale during the challenging early days.

GRADUAL INCREASE IN CUSTOMER BASE AND POPULARITY THROUGH WORD OF MOUTH

Their relentless hard work and commitment began to pay off. Slowly but surely, word of mouth started to spread about the delicious food and welcoming atmosphere at "Sibling Savors." Satisfied customers shared their positive experiences with friends and family, and online reviews praised both the cuisine and the service.

Local food bloggers and critics began to take notice. Positive reviews in newspapers and blogs brought new customers through the door. Max and Ash made sure to engage with their patrons, thanking them for their support and encouraging them to spread the word. They also continued to innovate, keeping the menu fresh and exciting to attract repeat customers.

Slowly, the Restaurant Started to Gain a Loyal Customer Base

As more people discovered "Sibling Savors," the restaurant started to build a loyal customer base. Regular patrons appreciated the consistently high quality of the food and the warm, friendly service. Max and Ash made it a point to remember their regulars' names and preferences, fostering a sense of community and belonging.

Events such as wine tastings, themed dinners, and live music nights further enhanced the restaurant's appeal. These events attracted new visitors and provided a platform for showcasing the creativity and versatility of Max's culinary talents.

The gradual increase in customer base translated into improved financial stability. Ash's careful management ensured that profits were reinvested into the business, allowing them to make necessary upgrades and improvements. The brothers began to see the fruits of their labor, and their dream of running a successful restaurant started to become a reality.

Looking Ahead

With "Sibling Savors" finally gaining traction, Max and Ash could start thinking about the future. They knew that maintaining their momentum required continuous innovation and unwavering dedication. They were ready to take on new challenges, expand their horizons, and bring their culinary vision to even more people. The journey had been tough, but their perseverance and hard work had laid a solid foundation for future success.

CHAPTER 4

EXPANSION AND NEW VENTURES

DECISION TO OPEN MORE RESTAURANTS

After achieving success with "Sibling Savors," Max and Ash began to entertain the idea of expanding their culinary empire. The positive feedback from customers and the financial stability they had finally achieved gave them the confidence to explore new opportunities. They realized that their skills and unique approach to food could be the foundation for a series of successful restaurants, each offering a different culinary experience.

They spent countless hours discussing their vision for expansion, identifying potential gaps in the market, and brainstorming concepts that would excite and attract food lovers. Their goal was not just to replicate the success of "Sibling Savors," but to introduce new and innovative dining experiences that would appeal to a wide range of palates.

SECOND RESTAURANT: "FUSION FLAVORS"

The concept for their second restaurant, "Fusion Flavors," was born out of Max's fascination with blending different culinary traditions and Ash's strategic market analysis. They decided to combine Asian and Latin American cuisines, creating a menu that offered a unique and exciting dining experience. This fusion approach allowed them to experiment with bold flavors and unconventional pairings, resulting in dishes that were both innovative and delicious.

"Fusion Flavors" Combined Asian and Latin American Cuisines, Offering a Unique and Exciting Dining Experience

The restaurant featured a vibrant and modern interior, with colorful decor that reflected the lively fusion of cultures. The menu included dishes like sushi tacos, miso-marinated pork belly with chimichurri, and tempura avocado with spicy mango salsa. These inventive creations quickly attracted food enthusiasts eager to try something new.

Max spent months perfecting the recipes, ensuring that each dish was a harmonious blend of the best elements from both cuisines. He worked closely with suppliers to source authentic ingredients, importing exotic spices and fresh produce to maintain the highest quality. Ash, meanwhile, focused on creating an engaging and efficient dining experience, training the staff to explain the unique menu items and provide excellent service.

The opening of "Fusion Flavors" was a resounding success. The innovative fusion of flavors captured the imagination of diners, and the restaurant received rave reviews from critics and customers alike. Food bloggers and influencers were quick to spread the word, and soon "Fusion Flavors" became a go-to spot for adventurous eaters.

THIRD RESTAURANT: "MEDITERRANEAN DELIGHTS"

Buoyed by the success of "Fusion Flavors," Max and Ash decided to embark on their third venture: "Mediterranean Delights." This restaurant focused on Greek and Italian cuisine, featuring fresh and flavorful dishes that celebrated the vibrant and healthy Mediterranean diet. They wanted to offer a dining experience that was both wholesome and indulgent, highlighting the natural flavors of high-quality ingredients.

"Mediterranean Delights" Focused on Greek and Italian Cuisine, Featuring Fresh and Flavorful Dishes

The restaurant's decor was inspired by the sun-soaked landscapes of the Mediterranean, with rustic wooden tables, whitewashed walls, and accents of blue and terracotta. The menu included classics like Greek moussaka, Italian risotto, grilled octopus with lemon and herbs, and handmade pasta with rich, savory sauces. Each dish was crafted to showcase the simplicity and depth of Mediterranean cooking.

Max drew on his extensive culinary training to create a menu that was both authentic and innovative. He traveled to Greece and Italy to study traditional cooking techniques and source specialty ingredients. The result was a menu that transported diners to the shores of the Mediterranean with every bite.

Ash once again took charge of the operational aspects, ensuring that "Mediterranean Delights" ran smoothly and efficiently. He implemented a robust inventory management system to handle the diverse range of ingredients and developed a comprehensive training program for the staff. Customer service was paramount, and Ash worked tirelessly to create a warm and inviting atmosphere that complemented the exceptional food.

The response to "Mediterranean Delights" was overwhelmingly positive. Health-conscious diners appreciated the focus on fresh, nutritious ingredients, while food lovers were drawn to the rich, satisfying flavors. The restaurant quickly became a favorite among those who appreciated the vibrant and healthy Mediterranean diet.

EMPHASIS ON SELECTING THE BEST INGREDIENTS AND CREATING PASSIONATE DISHES

At each of their restaurants, Max and Ash emphasized the importance of using high-quality ingredients and creating dishes with passion and creativity. They believed that the foundation of any great dish was the quality of its ingredients, and they spared no effort in sourcing the best produce, meats, and spices. They established strong relationships with local farmers and suppliers, ensuring a steady supply of fresh, seasonal ingredients.

Max's culinary philosophy was centered around the idea that cooking was an art form, a way to express creativity and passion. He approached each dish with meticulous attention to detail, striving to balance flavors, textures, and presentations. His dedication to excellence was evident in every bite, and diners could taste the care and effort that went into each meal.

Ash's expertise in business and hospitality complemented Max's culinary skills perfectly. He understood that a successful restaurant required more than just great food; it needed a seamless operation, outstanding customer service, and a compelling brand. Ash's strategic vision and leadership ensured that each restaurant not only met but exceeded customer expectations.

Innovative Menu Development

Max continuously innovated, developing new recipes and refining existing ones to keep the menus fresh and exciting. He hosted tasting sessions where the staff could provide feedback, fostering a collaborative environment that encouraged creativity and improvement. Seasonal specials and limited-time offerings kept diners coming back to see what new delights were on offer.

Operational Excellence and Customer Experience

Ash implemented systems and processes to maintain high standards across all aspects of the business. From efficient supply chain management to rigorous staff training, he ensured that each restaurant operated like a well-oiled machine. Customer feedback was taken seriously, with regular reviews and adjustments made to enhance the dining experience.

Building a Strong Brand and Community Presence

Max and Ash also focused on building a strong brand and community presence. They engaged with their customers through social media, sharing behind-the-scenes glimpses of the kitchen, announcing special events, and highlighting local partnerships. Community involvement was a priority, and they regularly hosted charity events and culinary workshops, giving back to the neighborhoods that supported them.

Looking Ahead

The expansion of Max and Ash's culinary empire was a testament to their vision, dedication, and complementary skills. From the success of "Sibling Savors" to the innovative offerings at "Fusion Flavors" and the vibrant dishes at "Mediterranean Delights," they proved that with passion and hard work, dreams could become reality. Their commitment to quality, creativity, and customer satisfaction set them apart in the competitive restaurant industry, establishing them as leaders and innovators in the culinary world. As they looked to the future, Max and Ash were excited about the possibilities, ready to continue their journey and inspire others with their story of success.

CHAPTER 5
RECOGNITION AND SUCCESS

RESTAURANTS BECOMING FAMOUS FOR GREAT FOOD AND EXCELLENT SERVICE

Max and Ash's dedication to their craft began to pay off as their restaurants quickly gained a stellar reputation. Word of mouth spread rapidly, and soon, their establishments were known far and wide for exceptional food and outstanding customer service. Max's culinary creativity and Ash's meticulous management created a dining experience that was both memorable and enjoyable.

Max and Ash's Restaurants Gained a Reputation for Their Exceptional Food and Outstanding Customer Service

"Sibling Savors" became a household name in their hometown and beyond. Patrons praised the delicious, unique dishes crafted by Max, who had a knack for turning ordinary ingredients into extraordinary meals. The warm and welcoming atmosphere cultivated by Ash made every visit a pleasant experience. Regulars appreciated the personal touch, with staff remembering their preferences and Max occasionally coming out to greet diners and discuss the menu.

The success of "Sibling Savors" was replicated with their other ventures. "Fusion Flavors" and "Mediterranean Delights" attracted food enthusiasts who were eager to explore the innovative fusion of Asian and Latin American cuisines or the fresh, vibrant flavors of the Mediterranean. The consistent quality of food and service across all their restaurants solidified their reputation as top-tier restaurateurs.

They Consistently Received Positive Reviews from Critics and Diners Alike

Food critics and bloggers took notice of Max and Ash's establishments. Articles and reviews highlighting the creativity of Max's dishes and the efficiency of Ash's management style appeared regularly. These positive reviews not only attracted new customers but also validated the brothers' hard work and commitment to excellence. Diners frequently left glowing comments on social media and review platforms, praising everything from the food to the ambiance to the attentive service.

WINNING AWARDS AND FEATURES IN FOOD MAGAZINES AND TV SHOWS

Their culinary talents and successful restaurant management earned Max and Ash numerous awards. "Sibling Savors" won local accolades for Best New Restaurant and Best Casual Dining, while "Fusion Flavors" received awards for Best Fusion Cuisine and Most Innovative Menu. "Mediterranean Delights" was celebrated for its authentic flavors and exceptional use of fresh ingredients, earning titles like Best Mediterranean Restaurant and Healthiest Menu.

Their Culinary Talents and Successful Restaurant Management Earned Them Numerous Awards

These awards were more than just trophies; they were symbols of recognition from the culinary world and their community. Max and Ash attended award ceremonies, where they met other industry leaders and exchanged ideas. Each award motivated them to continue pushing the boundaries of culinary creativity and excellence in service.

They Were Featured in Prominent Food Magazines and Appeared on Popular TV Shows, Further Boosting Their Profile

The brothers' success stories caught the attention of prominent food magazines such as Bon Appétit, Food & Wine, and Gourmet. These publications featured in-depth articles about their journey, their innovative approaches, and their unique restaurant concepts. These features brought national attention to their restaurants, drawing food tourists and gourmands eager to experience their acclaimed cuisine.

Max and Ash also made appearances on popular TV shows, where they demonstrated their cooking techniques and shared their story. Shows like "Top Chef," "Chopped," and "Iron Chef America" invited Max to compete, showcasing his skills to a broader audience. These appearances further boosted their profile, attracting a new wave of customers excited to dine at their restaurants.

MAX'S PARTICIPATION IN COOKING COMPETITIONS

Max's invitation to participate in various cooking competitions was a testament to his growing reputation as a top chef. These competitions were high-stakes events that brought together some of the best culinary talents from around the world. Max relished the challenge, seeing it as an opportunity to showcase his innovative dishes and learn from other top chefs.

Max Was Invited to Participate in Various Cooking Competitions, Showcasing His Innovative Dishes and Competing with Other Top Chefs

In one memorable competition, Max wowed the judges with his signature dish, a deconstructed sushi taco that combined the delicate flavors of Japanese cuisine with the bold spices of Latin America. His innovative approach and flawless execution earned him high praise and a coveted spot in the finals.

Max's participation in these competitions provided valuable exposure for their restaurants. Television broadcasts and media coverage highlighted his culinary creativity, drawing new customers who wanted to experience the food that had impressed the judges.

These Competitions Provided Valuable Exposure and Opportunities to Learn from Other Culinary Experts

Competing also allowed Max to network with other chefs and learn new techniques. He brought these new ideas back to their restaurants, constantly evolving and improving the menu. The lessons he learned and the relationships he built through these competitions were invaluable, contributing to the continued success of their culinary ventures.

ASH'S REPUTATION IN THE BUSINESS WORLD

While Max was gaining recognition in the culinary sphere, Ash was making a name for himself in the business community. His expertise in restaurant management, from efficient operations to strategic marketing, garnered respect and admiration from peers and industry leaders.

Ash Became a Respected Figure in the Business Community, Known for His Expertise in Restaurant Management

Ash's ability to turn culinary creativity into a profitable business model was widely acknowledged. He was invited to share his insights at business conferences and hospitality workshops, where he spoke about the intricacies of running a successful restaurant. His presentations were well-received, filled with practical advice and real-world examples drawn from their experiences.

He Was Invited to Speak at Conferences and Workshops, Sharing Insights on Running Successful Restaurants and Inspiring Aspiring Entrepreneurs

At these events, Ash often spoke about the importance of creating a cohesive brand, maintaining high standards of quality and service, and adapting to market trends. He shared stories of their early struggles, emphasizing the lessons learned and the strategies that led to their success. Ash's talks inspired many aspiring entrepreneurs, who saw him as a mentor and a role model.

His reputation as a knowledgeable and innovative business leader led to invitations to collaborate on industry panels, contribute to business journals, and mentor up-and-coming restaurateurs. Ash's influence extended beyond their restaurants, impacting the broader business community and setting new standards for excellence in restaurant management.

Looking Ahead

Max and Ash's journey from aspiring restaurateurs to industry leaders is a story of dedication, innovation, and success. Their restaurants became famous for exceptional food and outstanding service, consistently receiving positive reviews and accolades. Max's participation in cooking competitions and Ash's reputation in the business world further cemented their status as leaders in their respective fields.

Their achievements were recognized with numerous awards, features in prominent food magazines, and appearances on popular TV shows. Through their hard work and commitment to excellence, Max and Ash not only built a successful culinary empire but also inspired others to pursue their dreams with passion and perseverance.

As they continued to expand their ventures and influence, Max and Ash remained true to their values, always striving to deliver the best possible dining experience and give back to the community that supported them. Their story is a testament to the power of hard work, creativity, and the unbreakable bond between two brothers.

CHAPTER 6
GIVING BACK TO THE COMMUNITY

CREATION OF SCHOLARSHIPS FOR STUDENTS STUDYING COOKING OR HOSPITALITY

Max and Ash understood that the opportunity to pursue higher education in culinary arts and hospitality management had been crucial in their journey to success. They were committed to providing similar opportunities for aspiring chefs and hospitality professionals who lacked the financial resources to follow their dreams.

Max and Ash Established Scholarships to Support Students Pursuing Careers in Cooking or Hospitality

To this end, they established the "Sibling Savors Scholarship Fund." This scholarship was open to high school seniors and current college students who demonstrated a passion for the culinary arts or hospitality management. The selection process was rigorous, involving an application that included an essay, letters of recommendation, and an interview.

Max and Ash were personally involved in the selection process. They read every application and often visited schools to talk to students about their career aspirations. The scholarships covered tuition fees, books, and sometimes even living expenses, depending on the financial need of the recipient.

They Recognized the Importance of Education and Wanted to Give Others the Opportunity to Follow Their Dreams

The brothers wanted to ensure that deserving students had the chance to pursue their education without the burden of financial stress. By providing these scholarships, Max and Ash were not only helping students achieve their educational goals but also investing in the future of the culinary and hospitality industries. Many of the scholarship recipients went on to attend prestigious culinary schools and hospitality programs, and some even returned to work at Max and Ash's restaurants, bringing new skills and fresh perspectives.

ORGANIZING CHARITY EVENTS AND RAISING MONEY FOR LOCAL CAUSES

In addition to their scholarship fund, Max and Ash regularly organized charity events at their restaurants. These events were designed to raise funds for various local causes, from supporting schools and community centers to funding healthcare initiatives and environmental conservation efforts.

They Regularly Organized Charity Events at Their Restaurants to Raise Funds for Various Local Causes

One of their most successful events was the annual "Taste of Fusion" festival held at "Fusion Flavors." This event featured a variety of food stalls offering dishes from different chefs, live cooking demonstrations by Max, and live music performances. The festival drew large crowds and created a festive atmosphere. All proceeds from ticket sales and food purchases were donated to local schools to support educational programs and extracurricular activities.

Another significant event was the "Mediterranean Nights" dinner series at "Mediterranean Delights." These dinners showcased multi-course meals inspired by various Mediterranean countries. Each evening focused on a different country's cuisine, offering guests a unique dining experience. Proceeds from these dinners supported local cultural initiatives and art programs, fostering a deeper appreciation for diverse cultures within the community.

These Events Brought the Community Together and Highlighted the Restaurants' Commitment to Giving Back

These charity events were more than just fundraisers; they were community gatherings that brought people together. They created opportunities for social interaction and community building, reinforcing the sense of belonging and mutual support among the residents. The events also highlighted Max and Ash's commitment to giving back and their belief in the power of community.

DONATIONS TO LOCAL FOOD BANKS

Understanding the importance of addressing food insecurity, Max and Ash made it a priority to support local food banks. They believed that no one should go hungry, and they used their success to help those in need.

Max and Ash Also Donated a Portion of Their Profits to Local Food Banks, Helping to Support Those in Need and Fight Hunger in Their Community

They committed to donating a portion of their profits to local food banks on a regular basis. These donations helped food banks purchase necessary supplies and distribute food to families and individuals facing financial hardships. In addition to monetary contributions, Max and Ash organized food drives at their restaurants, encouraging customers and employees to donate non-perishable food items.

During the holiday season, they intensified their efforts to ensure that everyone in the community could enjoy festive meals. They partnered with food banks to create holiday meal packages, which included turkeys, fresh vegetables, and all the trimmings for a traditional holiday feast. Volunteers from their restaurants helped pack and distribute these meals, spreading holiday cheer and providing much-needed support to struggling families.

SHOWING GRATITUDE AND MAKING A POSITIVE IMPACT

Max and Ash's philanthropic efforts were deeply rooted in gratitude. They recognized that their success was made possible by the support of their community, and they were determined to give back in meaningful ways.

Through Their Philanthropic Efforts, Max and Ash Expressed Their Gratitude for the Support They Had Received and Made a Positive Impact on Their Community

Their contributions went beyond financial support. Max and Ash were actively involved in their initiatives, volunteering their time and skills to make a difference. They visited schools to talk about the importance of culinary education, hosted free cooking classes for underprivileged youth, and mentored young entrepreneurs.

Their commitment to making a positive impact was widely recognized and appreciated. The community saw Max and Ash not just as successful restaurateurs but as compassionate leaders dedicated to improving the lives of those around them. Their actions inspired others to get involved and support local causes, creating a ripple effect of kindness and generosity.

Legacy of Philanthropy

Max and Ash's philanthropic legacy extended beyond their immediate contributions. They established an annual charity gala, "The Savors Benefit," which brought together business leaders, community members, and celebrities to raise funds for various causes. This high-profile event became a cornerstone of their philanthropic efforts, raising significant amounts of money and drawing attention to important issues.

Through their sustained efforts, Max and Ash demonstrated that true success is measured not just by financial achievements but by the positive impact one can have on others. Their journey of giving back became an integral part of their story, reflecting their values and their unwavering commitment to their community.

Looking Ahead

Max and Ash's dedication to giving back to their community highlighted their belief in the importance of supporting others and fostering positive change. Through scholarships, charity events, and donations, they made significant contributions that helped many individuals and families. Their philanthropic efforts were a testament to their gratitude, compassion, and desire to make a lasting difference. As they continued to grow their culinary empire, Max and Ash remained committed to their mission of giving back, ensuring that their success benefited not just themselves but the entire community.

CHAPTER 7

FAMILY SUPPORT AND INFLUENCE

CHARLOTTE AND ASHER'S ADVICE AND ENCOURAGEMENT

From the very beginning of Max and Ash's culinary journey, their parents, Charlotte and Asher, were their biggest supporters. Charlotte and Asher had always believed in the importance of following one's passion and instilled these values in their children from a young age. They provided not only moral support but also practical advice that was instrumental in helping Max and Ash navigate the complexities of starting and running a business.

Their Parents, Charlotte and Asher, Provided Invaluable Advice and Encouragement Throughout Their Journey

Charlotte, who had a natural talent for nurturing and guiding her children, often spent time discussing Max and Ash's plans with them. She had a keen sense of when they needed a gentle push or a comforting word. She reminded them to maintain a balance between their professional ambitions and personal well-being, emphasizing the importance of self-care and mental health.

Asher, with his business acumen and experience, offered strategic advice on financial management, marketing, and operational efficiency. He helped them draft their initial business plan and provided insights into managing cash flow, negotiating with suppliers, and understanding market trends. His pragmatic approach complemented Charlotte's emotional support, giving Max and Ash a well-rounded foundation.

They Reminded Max and Ash to Stay True to Their Values and Remain Dedicated to Their Goals

Charlotte and Asher continuously emphasized the importance of staying true to their values. They reminded Max and Ash that success should not come at the expense of integrity, quality, or their passion for cooking. This advice became a guiding principle for the brothers, influencing every decision they made. Whether it was choosing suppliers who shared their commitment to sustainability or ensuring fair treatment of their staff, Max and Ash upheld the values instilled in them by their parents.

CLARA'S ASSISTANCE AT THE RESTAURANTS DURING BUSY TIMES

Clara, Max and Ash's sister, also played a crucial role in their journey. She was always ready to lend a hand during busy times, providing much-needed support that kept the restaurants running smoothly. Clara's involvement extended beyond just helping out; she brought a unique energy and perspective that enriched the family dynamic within the business.

Clara Often Helped Out at the Restaurants, Especially During Busy Periods, Providing Additional Support and Lending a Helping Hand

During peak seasons and special events, Clara could often be found working alongside the rest of the team. Whether it was greeting customers, serving dishes, or assisting in the kitchen, she was a reliable and enthusiastic presence. Her ability to connect with customers added a personal touch to the dining experience, fostering a sense of community and loyalty.

Clara's involvement was particularly invaluable during the launch of new ventures. When "Fusion Flavors" and "Mediterranean Delights" opened, she took on additional responsibilities to ensure a smooth start. She managed reservations, handled customer feedback, and even helped with marketing efforts by promoting the restaurants on social media and within her network. Her contributions were vital to the successful opening and operation of these establishments.

THE ROLE OF A STRONG FAMILY BOND IN KEEPING MAX AND ASH GROUNDED AND MOTIVATED

The strong bond within their family was a constant source of strength and motivation for Max and Ash. This bond provided a solid foundation that helped them navigate the inevitable challenges of running a business. The support they received from their parents and Clara was instrumental in maintaining their focus and drive.

The Strong Bond Within Their Family Kept Max and Ash Grounded and Motivated, Providing a Solid Foundation for Their Success

Regular family gatherings were a cherished tradition that kept everyone connected. These gatherings were an opportunity to share updates, celebrate milestones, and offer mutual support. They often turned into brainstorming sessions where Max and Ash would discuss new ideas and get feedback from their family. This open communication and collaborative spirit were crucial in fostering innovation and resilience.

The family's shared experiences also served as valuable lessons. Charlotte and Asher often recounted their own challenges and triumphs, providing context and perspective that helped Max and Ash understand the broader picture. These stories reinforced the importance of perseverance and adaptability, key qualities that contributed to their success.

They Celebrated Their Achievements Together and Supported Each Other Through Challenges

Celebrations of achievements were always a family affair. Whether it was winning an award, opening a new restaurant, or simply achieving a significant milestone, Max and Ash made sure to share these moments with their loved ones. These celebrations were not just about the accomplishments but also about recognizing the collective effort and support that made them possible.

During challenging times, the family rallied together, offering encouragement and practical help. When Max and Ash faced financial difficulties in the early days, Asher helped them restructure their budget and negotiate with suppliers. During slow business periods, Charlotte provided emotional support, reminding them of their progress and potential.

One particularly challenging period was when "Fusion Flavors" faced unexpected supply chain issues that threatened their ability to maintain menu consistency. Clara stepped in to manage customer communications, reassuring patrons and handling feedback with grace. Meanwhile, Asher used his business contacts to find alternative suppliers, and Charlotte provided a steadying influence, keeping everyone focused and positive.

Looking Ahead

The unwavering support and influence of their family were integral to Max and Ash's success. Charlotte and Asher's advice and encouragement, coupled with Clara's hands-on assistance, provided a strong foundation that kept them grounded and motivated. This family bond not only helped them achieve their goals but also enriched their journey, making their accomplishments even more meaningful. Max and Ash's story is a testament to the power of family support in overcoming challenges and achieving success.

LEGACY AND INSPIRATION

RESTAURANTS KNOWN FOR HIGH-QUALITY FOOD AND WELCOMING ATMOSPHERE

Max and Ash's restaurants, "Sibling Savors," "Fusion Flavors," and "Mediterranean Delights," each carved out a niche in the culinary world with their unique offerings and impeccable service. They became synonymous with high-quality food and a welcoming atmosphere, consistently drawing in diners who appreciated the effort and care put into every aspect of their dining experience.

Max and Ash's Restaurants Became Synonymous with High-Quality Food and a Welcoming Atmosphere

Each restaurant's success was a testament to Max's culinary genius and Ash's business acumen. "Sibling Savors" was celebrated for its homey, comforting dishes that reminded diners of family gatherings. "Fusion Flavors" wowed guests with its innovative blend of Asian and Latin American cuisines, while "Mediterranean Delights" offered a fresh, vibrant take on Greek and Italian classics. The meticulous attention to detail in both food preparation and presentation ensured that every meal was an event to be remembered.

Diners appreciated the warm, friendly environment fostered by the staff, who were trained to uphold the values that Max and Ash held dear: respect, kindness, and a genuine passion for food. The personal touches – from Max greeting diners and discussing the menu to Ash ensuring that every guest felt valued – created a loyal customer base that returned time and again.

CREATION OF A LEGACY IN THE CULINARY WORLD

Max and Ash's dedication to their craft and their community helped them create a lasting legacy in the culinary world. Their influence extended beyond their restaurants, shaping the broader food culture and setting new standards for excellence.

Their Dedication to Their Craft and Their Community Created a Lasting Legacy in the Culinary World

Their commitment to using high-quality, locally sourced ingredients not only supported local farmers but also set a trend for sustainable dining practices. Max's innovative recipes and willingness to push culinary boundaries earned him accolades and respect from his peers. His creations were frequently featured in culinary magazines, and he was often invited to speak at industry conferences, where he shared his insights and inspired fellow chefs.

Ash's expertise in restaurant management also left a significant mark. He developed efficient systems for inventory management, staff training, and customer service that became models for other restaurateurs. Ash's lectures and workshops on hospitality management were well-attended, and his published articles

provided valuable guidance to up-and-coming entrepreneurs.

They Were Respected Not Only for Their Culinary Skills but Also for Their Integrity and Commitment to Excellence

Max and Ash were revered not just for their culinary and business skills, but also for their integrity. They maintained high ethical standards in every aspect of their work, from fair employment practices to transparent dealings with suppliers. Their commitment to excellence was unwavering, and this consistency earned them the trust and admiration of their peers and patrons alike.

INSPIRATION FOR ASPIRING CHEFS AND ENTREPRENEURS

Max and Ash's journey from aspiring restaurateurs to industry leaders inspired many young chefs and entrepreneurs. Their story was one of passion, hard work, and perseverance, showing that with dedication, dreams could indeed become reality.

Max and Ash's Story Inspired Many Aspiring Chefs and Entrepreneurs to Pursue Their Own Dreams

Aspiring chefs looked up to Max as a mentor and role model. His journey from a curious young cook experimenting in his family kitchen to a celebrated chef running multiple successful restaurants was a source of inspiration. Max often took time to mentor young chefs, offering them internships at his restaurants and sharing his knowledge and experience. His cooking classes and workshops were highly sought after, providing hands-on training and insight into the culinary world.

Similarly, Ash's story motivated many budding entrepreneurs. His ability to turn culinary creativity into a profitable business model was widely admired. Ash frequently spoke at business schools and entrepreneurship forums, where he shared his strategies for success and encouraged others to pursue their passions. His message was clear: with a solid plan, hard work, and resilience, one could overcome obstacles and achieve great success.

Their Journey Demonstrated That with Passion, Hard Work, and Perseverance, It Is Possible to Achieve Great Success

Max and Ash's journey was not without challenges, but their unwavering commitment to their goals and their ability to adapt and innovate were key to their success. They showed that success in the culinary world required a blend of creativity, business savvy, and an unrelenting work ethic. Their story became a beacon of hope and motivation for many who aspired to follow in their footsteps.

REFLECTION ON THEIR JOURNEY AND FEELING OF PRIDE AND FULFILLMENT

As Max and Ash looked back on their journey, they felt a deep sense of pride and fulfillment. They had turned their childhood dream into a reality, building a successful restaurant empire that made a positive impact on their community and the culinary world.

Looking Back on Their Journey, Max and Ash Felt a Deep Sense of Pride and Fulfillment

Reflecting on their achievements, they remembered the early days of "Sibling Savors," the excitement and anxiety of opening "Fusion Flavors," and the careful planning and execution that went into

"Mediterranean Delights." Each step of the way had been a learning experience, and each challenge had made them stronger and more determined.

They took pride in the recognition they had received, from industry awards to glowing reviews from critics and customers. More importantly, they felt fulfilled by the positive impact their work had on their community. The scholarships they had established, the charity events they had organized, and the donations they had made to local food banks were all testament to their commitment to giving back.

They Had Turned Their Childhood Dream into a Reality, Building a Successful Restaurant Empire and Making a Positive Impact on Their Community

Max and Ash's journey was a testament to the power of dreams, hard work, and the support of a loving family. They had created a legacy that would be remembered and cherished, not just for the restaurants they built but for the lives they touched and the inspiration they provided to others. Their story was a shining example of what could be achieved with passion, dedication, and an unwavering belief in oneself.

Looking Ahead

Max and Ash's journey from childhood dreamers to successful restaurateurs is a story of inspiration, dedication, and community impact. Their restaurants, known for high-quality food and welcoming atmospheres, became beacons of excellence in the culinary world. Through their hard work, they created a lasting legacy and inspired countless aspiring chefs and entrepreneurs. Their reflections on their journey reveal a deep sense of pride and fulfillment, as they turned their dreams into reality and made a positive impact on their community. Their story will continue to inspire and motivate future generations, proving that with passion, hard work, and perseverance, anything is possible.

CHAPTER 9

CONTINUED SUCCESS AND IMPACT

MAX AND ASH'S CONTINUED SUCCESS AND IMPACT ON THE CULINARY WORLD

Max and Ash continued to thrive in the ever-evolving culinary world, expanding their restaurant empire with a blend of creativity, innovation, and a commitment to excellence. Their ability to adapt to new trends and their unwavering dedication to quality ensured their place at the forefront of the industry.

Max and Ash Continued to Thrive, Expanding Their Restaurant Empire and Innovating in the Culinary World

Their next venture, "Global Bites," was a bold step into the world of international cuisine. This restaurant featured a rotating menu of dishes from around the world, allowing diners to experience different cultures through food. Max's culinary team traveled extensively, gathering inspiration and authentic recipes, which they then recreated with a modern twist. This venture was a hit, drawing food enthusiasts from near and far eager to sample the ever-changing menu.

Ash, on the other hand, leveraged technology to streamline operations and enhance customer experience. He introduced a cutting-edge reservation system, a customer feedback app, and even experimented with virtual reality dining experiences, where guests could "travel" to different parts of the world while enjoying their meal. These innovations not only set their restaurants apart but also demonstrated their forward-thinking approach and commitment to staying ahead of the curve.

Their Ongoing Success and Impact on the Culinary Scene Ensured That Their Legacy Would Endure

Max and Ash's influence extended beyond their restaurants. Max published a series of bestselling cookbooks, sharing his unique recipes and culinary philosophy with a broader audience. These books were celebrated for their creativity and practical tips, inspiring home cooks and professional chefs alike.

Ash became a sought-after speaker and consultant in the hospitality industry. He shared his expertise at international conferences, helping other restaurateurs improve their operations and customer service. His business acumen and innovative ideas were highly respected, and his guidance helped many new ventures find their footing in the competitive restaurant industry.

ENDURING LEGACY CHERISHED FOR GENERATIONS

The legacy of Max and Ash's restaurants, built on passion, hard work, and family support, was destined to be cherished for generations to come. Their establishments became landmarks in their hometown and popular destinations for food lovers everywhere.

The Legacy of Max and Ash's Restaurants, Built on Passion, Hard Work, and Family Support, Would Be Cherished for Generations to Come

Their commitment to sustainability and community engagement continued to resonate with diners. Max and Ash expanded their farm-to-table initiatives, sourcing even more ingredients locally and supporting sustainable farming practices. They also increased their charitable efforts, establishing a foundation to support culinary education and food security initiatives worldwide.

Max and Ash's family also played a crucial role in preserving their legacy. Clara, who also sometimes got involved in the family business, brought her own children, Eric, Ginny, and Georgia, into the fold, teaching them the values and skills that had made their restaurants successful. This next generation, inspired by their uncles' achievements, showed great promise in continuing the family tradition of culinary excellence and community service.

Their Story Became a Part of the Local Lore, Inspiring Future Generations

The story of Max and Ash became an integral part of local lore, a source of inspiration and pride for the community. Their journey from humble beginnings to culinary stardom was frequently recounted at community events, in schools, and in local media. The "Sibling Savors" Scholarship Fund continued to support aspiring chefs and hospitality professionals, many of whom cited Max and Ash as their role models.

TESTAMENT TO THE POWER OF PERSEVERANCE, TEAMWORK, AND FAMILY SUPPORT

Max and Ash's journey was a testament to the power of perseverance, teamwork, and the unwavering support of family. Their success was built on a foundation of hard work, mutual respect, and a shared vision.

Max and Ash's Journey Was a Testament to the Power of Perseverance, Teamwork, and the Unwavering Support of Family

Their story highlighted the importance of staying true to one's passion and values, no matter the challenges faced. Max and Ash encountered numerous obstacles along the way – financial struggles, fierce competition, and the constant pressure to innovate. However, their ability to persevere and maintain their integrity ensured their success.

Max's culinary creativity and relentless pursuit of excellence, combined with Ash's strategic vision and operational expertise, created a powerful synergy. This partnership, grounded in mutual respect and a deep family bond, was the cornerstone of their achievements.

Their Success Story Highlighted the Importance of Staying True to One's Passion and Values, No Matter the Challenges Faced

Max and Ash's story also underscored the importance of giving back to the community. They never forgot the support they received during their journey and were committed to making a positive impact. Their philanthropic efforts, whether through scholarships, charity events, or donations to food banks, demonstrated their belief in the importance of supporting others and fostering a sense of community.

Conclusion

Max and Ash's continued success and impact on the culinary world ensured that their legacy would endure. Their restaurants, known for high-quality food and welcoming atmospheres, became icons of culinary excellence. Their dedication to their craft and their community created a lasting legacy that would be cherished for generations.

Their journey was a powerful testament to the power of perseverance, teamwork, and family support. They showed that with passion, hard work, and a commitment to one's values, it is possible to achieve great success and make a positive impact on the world.

Max and Ash's story will continue to inspire future generations, proving that dreams can indeed become reality with the right mix of determination, innovation, and love.

PART FIVE
FAMILY REUNION CRUISE – A STORY OF CONNECTION AND LOVE

INTRODUCTION

SETTING THE SCENE – FAMILY DRIFTING APART

Introduction to the Family's Busy Lives: Work, School, and Growing Up Have Pulled Them in Different Directions

Years passed, and over time, life had a way of pulling people in different directions. For Charlotte and Asher, it felt like their family had become a collection of individuals living parallel lives. The once tight-knit group, who used to spend every holiday and summer vacation together, had gradually drifted apart as life became busier and more demanding.

Clara, their eldest, had grown into a successful therapist and writer. With her own thriving practice and three young children, her days were filled with sessions, deadlines, and the ever-present responsibilities of motherhood. She loved her family deeply, but between juggling work and taking care of her children—Eric, Ginny, and Georgia—finding time to visit her parents and brothers had become increasingly difficult. Weekend get-togethers were often replaced with quick phone calls or texts, and the distance, though unintentional, began to widen.

Max and Ash, the twins, had their own lives as well. After achieving success in the restaurant industry, they were constantly busy managing their growing culinary empire. Their restaurants were thriving, but the long hours spent overseeing operations, developing new menus, and managing staff left little time for family gatherings. Both had recently entered serious relationships, and while they were happy, the demands of running a business often overshadowed their personal lives.

Even Charlotte and Asher found themselves caught up in the whirlwind of their own lives. Asher had taken on more responsibilities at work, and Charlotte had become involved in several community projects. Their days were filled with meetings, errands, and the everyday tasks that seemed to fill every waking moment. Although they spoke to their children regularly, it wasn't the same as the in-person connection they once cherished.

As time passed, the family gatherings that had once been a regular occurrence grew few and far between. Holidays were sometimes celebrated over video calls, and the once-vibrant family traditions began to fade. The joy of simply being together—sharing meals, laughing over old stories, and creating new memories—was slipping away.

Charlotte, the Matriarch, Recognizes the Need to Reconnect as a Family

Charlotte, the heart of the family, noticed the subtle changes before anyone else. She saw how life's demands were slowly eroding the closeness that had once defined them. She missed the lively dinners, the spontaneous visits, and the warmth of her children's presence. She longed for the days when they would gather in the living room, talking late into the night, when their connection was as strong as ever.

Charlotte understood that time waits for no one. Her children were growing older, and her grandchildren were reaching milestones faster than she could keep up with. She realized that if she didn't take action soon, the opportunity to bring everyone back together might pass. She knew that maintaining their bond required more than just occasional phone calls or holiday texts—it required quality time spent together, away from the distractions of daily life.

As she reflected on what could be done, Charlotte's mind began to drift toward an idea she had been toying with for a while: a family reunion. But not just any reunion. She wanted to do something special, something that would allow them to disconnect from the busyness of life and reconnect with each other. She imagined a setting where they could relax, have fun, and, most importantly, spend time together as a family.

Charlotte's Dream of a Family Reunion on a Luxurious Cruise Ship—A Journey to Bring Everyone Back Together and Create Unforgettable Memories

It was during one of those quiet afternoons at home that the idea crystallized in her mind: a cruise. A luxurious cruise ship seemed like the perfect setting for their reunion. A place where they could escape from their hectic schedules and immerse themselves in an environment that offered both adventure and relaxation. On a cruise, there would be no work emails, no phone calls pulling them away—just endless days on the open sea, with nothing to focus on but each other.

Charlotte envisioned her family on the ship, waking up to the sound of the ocean and spending their days exploring new places, lounging by the pool, and enjoying each other's company. She imagined family dinners with stunning views of the sunset, where they could share stories, laugh, and create new memories. She wanted this reunion to be more than just a vacation; she wanted it to be an experience that would rekindle the closeness they once shared.

Excited by the idea, Charlotte shared her dream with Asher, who immediately agreed that it was the perfect way to bring the family back together. They began planning, selecting a cruise that offered everything from adventurous excursions to relaxing spa treatments, ensuring there would be something for everyone to enjoy. The cruise ship they chose was a magnificent vessel, complete with towering decks, sparkling pools, fine dining, and a plethora of activities that would cater to both the children and the adults.

As the plans started to take shape, Charlotte's excitement grew. She could already picture the joy on her children's faces as they boarded the ship, the laughter that would fill the air as they sailed into the horizon.

This was her chance to bring her family back together, to remind them of the love and connection that had always been at the core of who they were.

Charlotte knew that this cruise would be more than just a trip; it would be a journey back to each other. A journey that would help them reconnect, heal any distance that had grown between them, and create memories that would last a lifetime. With the cruise booked and the plans in place, she eagerly anticipated the day they would set sail, ready to reunite her family on the open seas.

CHAPTER 1
PLANNING THE CRUISE

CHOOSING THE CRUISE SHIP

Charlotte and Asher wanted the family reunion to be perfect, so choosing the right cruise ship was crucial. They began their search with a clear vision in mind: the ship needed to offer a blend of adventure, relaxation, and opportunities for quality time together. They spent evenings side by side, browsing travel websites and reading reviews, carefully considering what each cruise line had to offer.

Charlotte was particularly focused on finding a ship that provided a range of activities. She knew that their family had diverse interests, and she wanted everyone to have something to look forward to. Max and Ash, with their entrepreneurial spirits, would likely enjoy the fine dining and cooking classes available on board, while Clara's children would need plenty of entertainment, like pools, water slides, and games to keep them busy. Asher, ever the planner, suggested that they also look for a ship with quiet spaces, like libraries and lounges, where they could retreat and unwind.

The cruise ship they eventually selected was nothing short of spectacular. With its towering decks that offered breathtaking views of the ocean, sparkling pools surrounded by sun loungers, and an endless array of activities, it was everything they had imagined and more. The ship featured state-of-the-art amenities, from world-class restaurants and spas to a theater showcasing Broadway-style performances. There was a kids' club for the younger family members, fitness centers, and even adventure excursions for the more daring travelers.

Charlotte was particularly drawn to the ship's focus on both adventure and relaxation. She envisioned mornings spent exploring new destinations and afternoons lounging by the pool with a book. There were opportunities for the family to bond over shared experiences, such as group excursions to nearby islands, snorkeling in crystal-clear waters, or taking cooking classes together to learn new recipes.

After weeks of research and discussions, Charlotte and Asher finally booked the cruise. They chose a weeklong journey that would take them to exotic destinations, offering a perfect balance of time at sea and shore excursions. The ship itself became a destination, with all its luxurious offerings ensuring that, even during the days spent sailing, the family would never run out of things to do.

BUILDING EXCITEMENT

With the cruise booked, the countdown to departure began, and the excitement within the family started to build. Charlotte and Asher could hardly contain their enthusiasm as they shared the news with their children. Clara, Max, and Ash were all thrilled at the idea of getting away from their busy lives and spending time together on the open sea.

As the departure date approached, the family group chats buzzed with activity. Clara's children, Eric, Ginny, and Georgia, were especially excited. They peppered their mother with questions about the ship —how big it was, what the pools looked like, and whether they would be able to eat as much ice cream as they wanted. Clara laughed at their eagerness but shared in their excitement, looking forward to the time away from her practice and the opportunity to reconnect with her family.

Max and Ash, despite their busy schedules running multiple restaurants, began clearing their calendars and preparing for the trip. For them, the cruise was not only a chance to relax but also an opportunity to reconnect with each other and the rest of the family. They exchanged messages about what they were looking forward to the most—Ash was excited about the chance to disconnect from work and spend quality time with his girlfriend, while Max looked forward to the culinary experiences on board.

Packing lists were drawn up, and conversations about what to bring became part of the daily family chatter. Charlotte and Asher sent links to helpful packing guides and recommended items that would make the trip more enjoyable. Charlotte even made sure to remind everyone to pack formal wear for the elegant dinners they would have together on the ship. She was determined to create moments of shared elegance and joy, where the family could dress up, enjoy gourmet meals, and bask in the beauty of the ocean around them.

The anticipation was palpable as the family imagined the destinations they would visit. Pictures of pristine beaches, lush rainforests, and bustling port cities were shared, sparking conversations about which excursions they wanted to join. Clara's children were eager to try snorkeling for the first time, while Max and Ash debated between a guided culinary tour in one port and a thrilling zipline adventure in another.

Asher, always the organizer, took on the role of creating a loose itinerary for their time aboard. He researched the ship's activities and suggested a few key moments where the whole family could gather—whether it was a group brunch on the deck, a trivia night, or simply stargazing after dinner. He wanted to make sure there was a balance of family time and personal space, ensuring that everyone could relax in their own way while still creating lasting memories together.

The excitement continued to build as departure day drew closer. Every conversation seemed to revolve around the upcoming cruise, and the sense of anticipation brought the family closer, even before they set foot on the ship. They could already feel the promise of adventure and relaxation waiting for them, and they knew that this reunion would be an unforgettable experience—one that would bring them back to what mattered most: each other.

CHAPTER 2
DEPARTURE DAY

ARRIVING AT THE PORT

The day had finally arrived. The morning was filled with a buzz of excitement and a hint of nervousness as the family members made their way to the bustling port, where the massive cruise ship awaited them. The harbor was alive with activity—passengers arriving with suitcases in tow, porters rushing back and forth, and the gleaming ship towering over the dock, its name emblazoned in elegant script along the side.

Charlotte and Asher were the first to arrive, standing near the entrance to the terminal with wide smiles on their faces as they watched the scene unfold. Charlotte clutched her boarding pass tightly, glancing around with a mix of anticipation and relief that the day had finally come. She looked over at Asher, who gave her a reassuring nod. This was the moment they had been waiting for—the culmination of weeks of planning and anticipation.

Soon, the rest of the family began to gather. Clara, now a successful therapist and writer, was the next to arrive, accompanied by her husband Alexander and their three children: Eric, Ginny, and Georgia. Clara, always composed and calm, was busy making sure that her children were accounted for as they excitedly pointed out the various features of the port—the cranes loading luggage, the towering cruise ship, and the throngs of other travelers.

Clara's husband Alexander, a steady and dependable presence, walked beside her, carrying most of the luggage and smiling at the children's enthusiasm. Eric, the oldest, was particularly eager, his eyes widening as he took in the size of the ship. Ginny and Georgia giggled as they chased each other around their parents, their excitement palpable. Clara exchanged a knowing smile with Charlotte as they approached, both mothers understanding the joy of seeing their children so full of energy and wonder.

A few minutes later, Max and Ash arrived, looking as charming as ever. Max, the head chef and co-owner of several restaurants, had a relaxed air about him, his eyes hidden behind a pair of sunglasses as he walked up to greet his parents. He was accompanied by his son, Jake, and girlfriend, Sophie, a fellow chef, who had a lively spirit that matched Max's passion for food. Sophie greeted everyone with warmth, immediately making the children laugh with her playful banter.

Ash, always the more business-minded of the two, took a confident stride as he approached with his daughter, Susan, and girlfriend, Emily, by his side. Emily, an event planner, exuded grace and calmness, perfectly complementing Ash's ambitious nature. Together, they made a striking couple, effortlessly navigating through the crowds as they joined the family.

As the family gathered together at the port, there was a palpable sense of reunion. Hugs were exchanged, luggage was shuffled around, and stories were quickly shared about the hectic morning preparations. The excitement was infectious as they stood in a group, gazing up at the massive ship that would be their home for the next week.

FIRST IMPRESSIONS OF THE SHIP

The cruise ship was a marvel of modern engineering and luxury. Standing tall with multiple decks stacked one on top of the other, it gleamed in the sunlight, its sleek design making it look like a floating city. The family members stared in awe at its sheer size, craning their necks to take it all in. From their vantage point, they could see balconies lining the upper decks, large pools filled with sparkling water, and a glass atrium that offered a glimpse of the lavish interior.

As they approached the boarding area, the grandeur of the ship became even more apparent. Charlotte, who had meticulously chosen this particular cruise, couldn't help but feel a sense of pride as she saw her family's expressions of amazement. This was exactly what she had hoped for—a place so grand and magnificent that it would immediately draw them in, capturing their imaginations and pulling them away from the stresses of their daily lives.

The family lined up to board, handing over their boarding passes and stepping onto the gangway that led to the ship. The moment they set foot on board, they were greeted by the ship's crew, who welcomed them with bright smiles and offered refreshments. The air was filled with the faint hum of excitement, as families and couples, all embarking on their own journeys, mingled and explored their new surroundings.

As they walked through the grand atrium, the family couldn't help but be in awe of the ship's interior. It was like stepping into a five-star hotel, with polished marble floors, towering glass elevators, and chandeliers that sparkled like stars. The atrium led to various decks, each offering a different experience—restaurants with gourmet cuisine, lounges with panoramic ocean views, and shops filled with high-end goods. The children were especially excited to spot the ice cream stations and pool areas, while the adults marveled at the sheer luxury of it all.

A sense of adventure filled the air as the family began to explore the ship. They found their rooms, each one elegantly designed with plush bedding, private balconies, and breathtaking views of the ocean. As they unpacked and settled in, the reality of the trip began to sink in. This was their time to disconnect from the outside world, to focus on each other and the experiences they would share over the next week.

Charlotte and Asher stood on their balcony for a moment, taking in the vastness of the ocean stretching out before them. Charlotte squeezed Asher's hand, her heart swelling with joy. They had done it. They had brought their family back together, and now, they were about to embark on a journey that would not only create new memories but also strengthen the bonds that had always held them together.

With everyone settled in, the ship's horn sounded, signaling their departure. The family gathered on the deck, watching as the port began to fade into the distance and the open sea spread out before them. The excitement in the air was almost tangible as the ship picked up speed, slicing through the waves, and carrying them toward new adventures and cherished moments that awaited them on this unforgettable family reunion.

CHAPTER 3
SETTLING INTO CRUISE LIFE

FINDING THE RHYTHM OF CRUISE LIFE

After the initial excitement of boarding the ship and exploring their new surroundings, the family quickly began to fall into the soothing rhythm of cruise life. The ship's gentle rocking as it cut through the waves, the endless horizon, and the sheer luxury of the experience created a peaceful atmosphere that allowed everyone to relax and let go of the stresses of their everyday lives.

Mornings Spent on the Deck Watching the Sunrise

Mornings on the cruise became a cherished time for the family. Charlotte, always an early riser, loved nothing more than sitting on the deck with a cup of coffee, watching the sunrise over the endless expanse of the ocean. Asher would often join her, and together they would enjoy the quiet moments of dawn, the sky painted in shades of pink, orange, and gold. They talked about how much they had missed these peaceful moments together, free from the rush of their daily routines.

Soon, Clara began to join her parents on these early morning outings. She found that the calm of the ocean and the beauty of the sunrise gave her the perfect space to reflect and recharge, away from the demands of her practice and the responsibilities of motherhood. Sometimes, Max and Ash would make their way to the deck as well, bringing their girl-friends along for a quiet stroll or a light breakfast as they enjoyed the cool morning breeze.

Afternoons Filled with Activities

As the day progressed, the family would come together for various activities. The cruise ship offered an impressive array of options, from swimming and water sports to cooking classes and trivia competitions. The children—Eric, Ginny, and Georgia—were thrilled by the ship's offerings. They would spend hours darting between the different pools, trying out the water slides, and indulging in as much ice cream as they could manage. The ship's kids' club quickly became their favorite spot, where they made new friends and participated in scavenger hunts, arts and crafts, and interactive games.

The adults, meanwhile, found themselves embracing the luxury and relaxation that the cruise provided. For Clara, Alexander, Max, Ash, and their partners, it was a rare opportunity to unwind. They spent their afternoons lounging by the pool, indulging in spa treatments, or simply enjoying the pleasure of doing nothing at all. Ash and Emily explored the ship's fitness center together, while Max and Sophie took a cooking class where they learned to prepare exotic dishes from the ship's head chef. Clara and Alexander often found quiet corners of the ship to sit and read or engage in deep conversations that strengthened their already strong bond.

Charlotte and Asher relished the chance to reconnect with their children as adults. They spent their after-noons moving between different family members, sometimes joining the kids in a game of mini-golf or accompanying the adults for a wine-tasting session. Each moment felt like a treasure, a gift of time and presence that reminded them of how important it was to stay connected, no matter how busy life became.

BONDING THROUGH ACTIVITIES

Highlights of Family Activities

One of the highlights of the trip was the time spent together as a family. The ship's activities gave them endless opportunities to bond, rediscovering the joy of being in each other's company. From swimming together in the pool to challenging each other to friendly games of ping pong, there was always something to do that brought laughter and joy.

The ship's expansive layout meant that there were countless places to explore. The family took time to wander through the different decks, marveling at the shops, theaters, and art galleries onboard. They spent an entire afternoon playing miniature golf on the top deck, surrounded by the ocean on all sides, and even tried their luck at the ship's casino, where Clara managed to win a small prize, much to everyone's delight.

The children loved the game room, filled with arcade machines, air hockey, and even a virtual reality experience that they couldn't get enough of. Charlotte and Asher found themselves being pulled into games of shuffleboard with the grandchildren, laughing as the competitive spirit of the family shone through in even the simplest of games.

Conversations and Shared Laughter as They Rediscover the Joy of Being Together

Perhaps the most meaningful moments of the trip were the quieter ones, where the family gathered around a table or sat on lounge chairs, simply talking and laughing. It was in these moments that they rediscovered the joy of being together, free from the distractions of work, school, and the routines that usually kept them apart.

During dinners, the conversation flowed easily as they shared stories from their lives—Clara talked about her latest book project, Max and Sophie shared tales from their restaurant ventures, and Ash excitedly discussed new business ideas with Emily's input. The children chimed in with their own adventures, recounting their excitement from the day's activities and their growing list of favorite spots on the ship.

There were times when they reminisced about the past—family vacations from years ago, funny moments from the children's childhoods, and even the challenges they had faced together. These conversations served as a reminder of the strength of their bond, of the love that had always held them together through both good times and bad.

Evenings often found them gathered on the deck, watching the sunset and enjoying the peacefulness that settled over the ship as the day came to a close. With drinks in hand, they shared their hopes for the future, their dreams, and their gratitude for being able to experience this journey together. The laughter that filled the air was genuine, and the connections that had frayed over time began to weave together again, stronger than before.

As the days passed, the family found a rhythm that was both comfortable and rejuvenating. The cruise allowed them to reconnect not just as individuals, but as a family. They had time to enjoy each other's company, time to laugh, and time to simply be present with one another. The ship became more than just a vessel; it became a sanctuary where they could rediscover the joy of being together, away from the pressures of everyday life.

CHAPTER 4

THE SPECIAL FAMILY DINNER

PLANNING A MEMORABLE DINNER

As the cruise progressed and the family began to settle into the relaxing rhythm of ship life, Charlotte and Asher decided it was time to create an evening that would be the highlight of their trip. The days had been filled with laughter, adventures, and bonding, but Charlotte wanted to carve out a moment that would bring them all together in a more intimate setting—a special dinner that would allow them to celebrate their journey as a family.

Charlotte and Asher poured over the ship's dining options, finally settling on a restaurant that promised a combination of exquisite cuisine and breathtaking views. The restaurant was perched on one of the highest decks of the ship, offering panoramic views of the ocean. With large glass windows that allowed the sunlight to pour in and a terrace that opened up to the sea breeze, it was the perfect spot for a sunset dinner. Charlotte envisioned her family sitting around the table, bathed in the golden light of the setting sun, sharing stories and creating new memories.

To make the evening even more special, Charlotte and Asher coordinated with the restaurant's staff to arrange a private dining experience. They reserved a long table near the terrace, ensuring they had an unobstructed view of the sunset. They also requested a menu that featured some of the ship's finest dishes, with options for everyone's tastes—delicate seafood, tender steaks, and vegetarian dishes that celebrated the fresh flavors of the season. For dessert, Charlotte asked for something truly special: a selection of decadent treats that would end the evening on a sweet note.

Charlotte and Asher worked together to keep the dinner a surprise for the rest of the family, wanting to create a moment that would not only be memorable but also feel like a gift—a reminder of how much they valued the time they were spending together. They made sure that every detail was perfect, from the seating arrangement to the wine selection, knowing that this dinner would be a chance to reflect on the family's journey and celebrate the bond that had held them together through the years.

THE DINNER

When the evening of the dinner arrived, Charlotte and Asher gathered the family together and led them to the restaurant. As they stepped inside, the family members were immediately struck by the beauty of the space. The soft glow of the setting sun filled the room, casting a warm light over everything. The windows offered a stunning view of the ocean, where the sky was beginning to turn shades of pink and orange as the sun dipped toward the horizon. The sight was breathtaking, and for a moment, everyone stood in awe, taking it all in.

As they were seated at the elegantly set table, the atmosphere was filled with a sense of anticipation and joy. The family knew that this dinner was special, and they could feel the love and care that Charlotte and Asher had put into planning it. The setting was perfect—the sound of the ocean in the background, the soft clinking of glasses as waitstaff moved gracefully around the room, and the laughter that bubbled up as the family settled into their seats.

The evening began with appetizers that were as beautiful as they were delicious. The presentation of each dish was impeccable, and the flavors were vibrant and fresh. Conversation flowed easily as they shared bites of food and talked about the highlights of the trip so far. The children were excited to recount their adventures, from splashing in the pool to exploring the ship's various attractions. The adults laughed as they shared their own experiences, each story adding to the collective memory of this once-in-a-lifetime journey.

As the sun continued to set, the main courses arrived, and the family savored each bite of the expertly prepared dishes. The food was exquisite, but it was the company that made the meal truly unforgettable. There was something magical about sitting together, surrounded by the endless ocean, with nothing to do but enjoy each other's presence. The worries and responsibilities of their lives on land felt far away, and in this moment, all that mattered was the love they shared as a family.

Asher's Toast

As the meal began to wind down and dessert was brought to the table—an array of decadent sweets that made everyone's eyes light up—Asher stood up, gently tapping his glass to get the family's attention.

The room quieted, and all eyes turned to him as he prepared to make a toast. Asher wasn't usually one for grand speeches, but tonight, he felt compelled to express the emotions that had been building in his heart since the start of the cruise.

"I want to thank each of you for being here," Asher began, his voice steady but filled with emotion. He looked around the table, meeting the eyes of his children, his grandchildren, and his wife, Charlotte, who smiled at him encouragingly. "This cruise isn't just a vacation; it's a celebration of the family we've built together. We've had our ups and downs, but through it all, we've stayed together. And that's something worth celebrating."

He paused for a moment, taking a breath as he gathered his thoughts. "I'm so proud of each of you—Clara, Max, Ash, you've all grown into such remarkable people. You've followed your passions, built your own lives, and still, you've remained connected to this family. That means more to me than I can put into words."

Asher's voice grew softer as he continued, the weight of his emotions evident in every word. "And to Charlotte—my partner in everything—I couldn't have done any of this without you. You are the heart of this family, the one who holds us all together."

Tears welled up in Charlotte's eyes as she listened to Asher's words. She reached across the table to squeeze his hand, her heart full of love and gratitude. The children, too, were visibly moved by their father's sincerity. There was a moment of quiet, the kind of silence that speaks volumes, as everyone reflected on the meaning behind Asher's words.

Emotional Responses from Charlotte and the Children

Clara, always thoughtful and composed, was the first to respond. She raised her glass and said, "To family —to the love that binds us and the memories we've shared. No matter where life takes us, I know that this bond will always be there, keeping us strong."

Max and Ash followed suit, raising their glasses in silent agreement. They, too, were moved by their father's words and by the realization of how much this time together meant. It wasn't just about the trip itself—it was about the deeper connection that had been rekindled, the love that had always been there, even when life pulled them in different directions.

As they clinked their glasses together, the sound echoed through the room, a symbol of their unity and love. The moment was simple, yet profound—a reminder of what truly mattered. They had all achieved so much in their individual lives, but this—this shared experience, this bond as a family—was the greatest achievement of all.

The rest of the evening passed in a blur of laughter, shared stories, and sweet indulgences. The family lingered at the table long after dessert had been served, savoring the time they had together. Outside, the sun had long since set, and the stars were beginning to twinkle in the night sky. But inside the restaurant, the warmth of the family's love shone brighter than any constellation.

As they finally stood to leave, there was a sense of contentment that filled the air. This dinner, this moment of reflection and celebration, had brought them even closer together. It was a night they would remember for years to come—a reminder that no matter where life took them, they would always have each other.

CHAPTER 5

SPECIAL MOMENTS ON THE CRUISE

CREATING LASTING MEMORIES

The days on the cruise passed like a dream, filled with moments that would be etched in the family's memories forever. There were many highlights, each one contributing to the magic of the trip and the joy of being together.

One of the most enchanting nights was spent dancing under the stars. The cruise ship hosted a special event on the top deck—a night of live music and dancing beneath the open sky. Charlotte and Asher, reminiscing about their younger days, took to the dance floor with grace and ease, moving in perfect sync as the music played. Watching their parents dance so effortlessly, Clara, Max, and Ash couldn't help but smile. Inspired by the scene, Max pulled Sophie onto the dance floor, followed by Ash and Emily, and soon enough, even Clara and Alexander joined in. The children, too, were spinning and twirling around, laughing as they tried to mimic the adults. The night was filled with the sound of music and laughter, the stars shining brightly above them as they danced late into the evening. It was a moment that felt timeless, as if the worries of the world had vanished, leaving only joy and love in their place.

The most cherished and unforgettable experiences were their days exploring the cruise's small, picturesque island destinations known for their white sandy beaches, crystal-clear waters, and stunning natural beauty. The half-day excursions were filled with adventure, relaxation, and bonding, allowing them to reconnect and feel closer than ever. The excursions included San Juan, Puerto Rico; Punta Cana, Dominican Republic; Oranjestad, Aruba; Willemstad, Curacao; Kralendijk, Bonaire; Castries, St. Lucia; and Basseterre, St. Kitts.

1. San Juan, Puerto Rico

- **Snorkeling Adventure:**

The day began with a short boat ride out to La Parguera Nature Reserve, a hidden gem along Puerto Rico's southern coast. The family eagerly donned their snorkeling gear and plunged into the crystal-clear waters. The underwater world was teeming with life, with vibrant coral reefs swaying gently in the current. Clara's children, Eric, Ginny, and Georgia, were especially thrilled as they swam alongside schools of colorful fish, their faces lighting up with excitement each time a sea turtle glided past or a playful dolphin surfaced nearby. The experience was mesmerizing, offering a close-up view of the beauty and diversity of marine life in this pristine environment.

- **Hiking in El Yunque Rainforest:**

After their snorkeling adventure, the family headed inland to El Yunque National Forest, the only tropical rainforest in the U.S. National Forest System. The hike through El Yunque was like stepping into another world—lush, green, and alive with the sounds of nature. The trail led them past towering trees, vibrant tropical flowers, and cascading waterfalls that seemed straight out of a postcard. The air was filled with the sweet scent of blooming orchids and the soothing sound of water rushing over rocks. As they walked, the family marveled at the biodiversity around them, spotting brightly colored birds and even a few playful coquí frogs. The hike was both invigorating and peaceful, a perfect way to connect with nature.

- **Beachside Picnic:**

Their next stop was Condado Beach, a beautiful stretch of sand known for its lively atmosphere and stunning views of the Atlantic Ocean. The family found a cozy spot under the shade of a palm tree, where they laid out a picnic of fresh seafood dishes prepared with local ingredients. The meal was a feast for the senses—juicy grilled shrimp, tender lobster tails, and a variety of tropical fruits bursting with flavor. Everyone raved about the freshness of the food, and there was plenty of laughter as they shared stories and enjoyed the warm sea breeze. It was a simple, yet perfect moment that encapsulated the essence of their island adventure.

- **Sunset on the Beach:**

As the day drew to a close, the family remained on the beach, watching the sun dip below the horizon. The sky was ablaze with shades of orange, pink, and purple, creating a breathtaking backdrop for their evening. The children played in the sand while the adults relaxed, reflecting on the day's experiences. The sound of the waves gently lapping at the shore provided a soothing soundtrack to the moment, and as darkness fell, they felt a deep sense of contentment. It was a day that had brought them closer together, filled with beauty, adventure, and love.

2. Punta Cana, Dominican Republic

- **Snorkeling in Bavaro Beach:**

The family's adventure in Punta Cana began with snorkeling at Bavaro Beach, a spot renowned for its turquoise waters and vibrant marine life. The children were beyond excited as they slipped into the water, eager to explore the coral reefs just below the surface. As they swam, they encountered a dazzling array of marine creatures—colorful fish darting in and out of coral formations, graceful sea turtles gliding by, and even a few curious dolphins who seemed to enjoy playing with their human visitors. The experience was magical, leaving the children with wide smiles and a sense of wonder at the underwater world.

- **Exploring the Indigenous Eyes Ecological Park:**

After snorkeling, the family took a short drive to the Indigenous Eyes Ecological Park, a protected reserve filled with lush greenery and hidden lagoons. The park's name comes from the crystal-clear freshwater lagoons, known as "eyes" by the Taino Indians. The family embarked on a peaceful hike through the park, following trails that wound through the dense tropical forest. Along the way, they discovered several of the park's lagoons, each more beautiful than the last, with waters so clear that they could see fish swimming below the surface. The tranquility of the park was a stark contrast to the bustling beach, providing a moment of quiet reflection and connection with nature.

- **Beachside Lunch:**

Their hike worked up an appetite, and the family was ready for lunch. They found a charming beachside restaurant that served traditional Dominican cuisine.

The meal was a highlight of the day—plump, juicy lobsters, tender fish fillets, and a variety of tropical sides, all bursting with flavor. The food was so fresh that it seemed to melt in their mouths, and the adults couldn't help but savor every bite. The children, too, enjoyed the meal, especially the sweet plantains and fresh coconut water. As they ate, they soaked in the view of the ocean, enjoying the gentle sea breeze and the sound of the waves crashing against the shore.

- **Relaxation by the Water:**

The afternoon was spent in pure relaxation. The family returned to Bavaro Beach, where they lounged on sunbeds, the warmth of the sun soaking into their skin. Some dozed off under the shade of an umbrella, while others waded back into the water for one last swim. The children built sandcastles, their laughter filling the air, while the adults chatted and reflected on the day's adventures. The peacefulness of the moment was exactly what they needed—a time to unwind, to let go of the stresses of everyday life, and to simply enjoy the beauty of their surroundings.

3. Oranjestad, Aruba

- **Snorkeling at Mangel Halto Reef:**

Aruba greeted the family with its signature sunny weather and warm hospitality. The day's first adventure took them to Mangel Halto Reef, a snorkeling spot known for its shallow, crystal-clear waters and vibrant marine life. As they entered the water, they were immediately captivated by the colorful corals and the array of sea creatures that called this reef home. The family swam together, pointing out schools of fish that sparkled in the sunlight and sea anemones that waved gently in the current. The water was so clear that it felt like they were swimming in an aquarium, with every detail of the underwater world visible. The experience was both exhilarating and serene, a perfect start to their day in Aruba.

- **Hiking in Arikok National Park:**

After their morning of snorkeling, the family set out to explore Arikok National Park, a vast area that covers nearly 20 percent of the island. The park's unique desert-like landscape was a stark contrast to the lush greenery they had seen in other destinations, with towering cacti, rugged terrain, and ancient limestone caves. The hike was a fascinating journey through Aruba's natural history, as they encountered striking geological formations and panoramic views of the island. The children were especially intrigued by the rock paintings left by the island's indigenous people, a reminder of Aruba's rich cultural heritage. The hike was challenging at times, but the stunning views and the sense of adventure made it all worthwhile.

- **Beachside Dining at Eagle Beach:**

As the afternoon approached, the family made their way to Eagle Beach, one of Aruba's most famous stretches of sand. Under the shade of a palm tree, they enjoyed a beachside picnic that featured freshly caught fish, grilled to perfection, and a selection of tropical fruits. The food was simple yet delicious, a true taste of Aruba's local flavors. Everyone raved about the meal, and there was a relaxed, joyful atmosphere as they ate, the sound of the ocean providing the perfect background music. After lunch, they took a stroll along the beach, their feet sinking into the soft, powdery sand as they admired the clear, turquoise waters.

- **Sunset Serenity:**

The day concluded with a serene moment on Eagle Beach, watching one of Aruba's famous sunsets. The sky transformed into a canvas of brilliant colors—deep oranges, pinks, and purples—reflecting on the water and casting a golden glow over the sand. The family gathered together, some sitting on the sand, others standing with their arms around each other, all silently taking in the beauty of the moment. The sunset was more than just a visual spectacle; it was a symbol of the peace and contentment they had found on this trip. As the last rays of sunlight disappeared below the horizon, they felt a deep sense of connection, both to each other and to the natural world around them.

4. Willemstad, Curacao

- **Snorkeling at Playa PortoMari:**

The vibrant island of Curacao welcomed the family with open arms, and their day began with a snorkeling adventure at Playa PortoMari. The beach, known for its calm waters and stunning coral reefs, was the perfect spot for exploring the underwater world. As the family snorkeled, they were surrounded by a kaleidoscope of colors—parrotfish, angelfish, and butterflyfish swam gracefully around them, while the coral formations provided a stunning backdrop. The children were especially delighted by the friendly parrotfish that seemed to follow them, its bright colors making it a favorite among the group. The beauty of the reef and the diversity of marine life made this snorkeling experience one of the highlights of their trip.

• Hiking through Christoffel National Park:

After their morning in the water, the family headed to Christoffel National Park, the largest national park in Curacao. The hike through the park was a journey through the island's natural and cultural history, with trails that led them through dense forests, open plains, and up to panoramic viewpoints. Along the way, they encountered rare plants and local wildlife, including the endangered Curacao white-tailed deer. The trail also took them past historical sites, such as old plantation ruins and ancient rock formations, adding a layer of intrigue to their adventure. The hike was peaceful, with only the sounds of nature accompanying them as they explored the park's diverse landscapes.

- **Curacao Cuisine Experience:**

After their hike, the family was ready for a well-deserved meal, and they found the perfect spot at a seaside restaurant in Willemstad. The menu featured fresh seafood dishes infused with Caribbean flavors, and the family eagerly dug in. The dishes were a celebration of Curacao's culinary traditions—grilled fish seasoned with local spices, conch fritters with a zesty dipping sauce, and tropical fruit salads that added a refreshing touch to the meal. The food was as vibrant as the island itself, and everyone agreed that this was one of the best meals of the trip. As they ate, they enjoyed the view of the ocean, the sound of the waves providing a soothing background to their meal.

- **Evening on the Beach:**

The day ended with a quiet moment on the sand, where the family gathered to watch the sunset. The beach was peaceful, with only a few other visitors scattered along the shore. As the sun began to set, the sky filled with soft pastel colors, and the family found themselves reflecting on the day's adventures. There was a sense of calm and contentment in the air, as they sat together, watching the sun dip below the horizon. The beauty of the moment was not lost on them, and they knew that this was another memory they would cherish for years to come.

5. Kralendijk, Bonaire

- **Snorkeling at Bonaire National Marine Park:**

Bonaire, known for its commitment to marine conservation, offered the family a unique snorkeling experience at its National Marine Park. The water was so clear that they could see the vibrant coral reefs and schools of tropical fish even before they entered the water. Once in, they were immediately surrounded by a stunning array of marine life—brightly colored fish darting in and out of coral formations, graceful sea turtles gliding by, and even the occasional stingray passing silently below. The children were captivated by the beauty of the reef, their faces lighting up with excitement as they explored this underwater paradise. The experience was both awe-inspiring and humbling, a reminder of the importance of preserving the natural world.

- **Exploring Washington Slagbaai National Park:**

After their morning of snorkeling, the family set out to explore Washington Slagbaai National Park, a rugged nature reserve that covers much of Bonaire's northern coast. The park's landscape was a striking contrast to the lush greenery they had seen on other islands, with arid terrain, rocky cliffs, and cacti as far as the eye could see. The hike through the park provided stunning views of the coastline, with the deep blue of the Caribbean Sea contrasting against the desert-like landscape. Along the way, they encountered flamingos in their natural habitat, their pink feathers standing out against the salt flats. The park was a reminder of the diversity of Bonaire's ecosystems, and the hike was a rewarding experience for everyone.

- **Beach Picnic:**

The family's next stop was a secluded beach within the park, where they enjoyed a beachside meal featuring freshly grilled seafood. The food was simple yet delicious, with the fresh flavors of the sea perfectly complemented by local spices and herbs. As they ate, they marveled at the beauty of their surroundings—the clear, turquoise waters, the soft, white sand, and the rugged cliffs that framed the beach. The meal was a highlight of the day, a chance to relax and enjoy the simple pleasures of good food and good company.

- **Sunset Views:**

As the day came to a close, the family gathered on the beach to watch the sunset. The sky was painted in shades of pink, orange, and purple, casting a warm glow over the water. The waves gently lapped at the shore, creating a soothing rhythm that matched the peacefulness of the moment. The family sat together, quietly reflecting on the day's adventures and the beauty of Bonaire. It was a moment of pure serenity, a perfect ending to a perfect day.

6. Castries, St. Lucia

- **Snorkeling at Anse Chastanet:**

St. Lucia welcomed the family with its stunning natural beauty, and their day began with snorkeling at Anse Chastanet, a beach known for its vibrant coral reefs and crystal-clear waters. The children were especially excited to explore the underwater world, and they were not disappointed. As they snorkeled, they encountered a dazzling array of marine life—brightly colored fish, delicate sea fans, and even a few playful sea turtles. The coral reefs were teeming with life, and the children's faces lit up with wonder as they swam among the fish. The experience was a highlight of the trip, a chance to see the beauty of St. Lucia's marine ecosystems up close.

- **Hiking to the Pitons:**

After their morning of snorkeling, the family set out on a hike to one of St. Lucia's most iconic landmarks—the Pitons. The twin volcanic peaks, rising majestically from the sea, provided a stunning backdrop for their hike. The trail was challenging at times, but the breathtaking views made it all worthwhile. As they climbed higher, they were rewarded with panoramic vistas of the island, with the lush greenery of the rainforest stretching out below them and the deep blue of the Caribbean Sea in the distance. The hike was a memorable adventure, a chance to connect with nature and experience the beauty of St. Lucia's landscape.

- **Fresh Seafood Lunch:**

After their hike, the family was ready for a well-deserved meal, and they found the perfect spot at a local restaurant that specialized in fresh seafood. The menu featured a variety of dishes made with locally sourced ingredients, and the family eagerly dug in. The flavors were bold and vibrant, a celebration of St. Lucian cuisine. The grilled fish, seasoned with local spices, was a favorite among the group, and the tropical fruit salads provided a refreshing contrast. As they ate, they enjoyed the view of the ocean, the sound of the waves providing a soothing background to their meal.

- **Relaxation on the Beach:**

The day ended with a relaxing evening on the beach, where the family gathered to watch the sunset. The sky was filled with brilliant colors, and the family sat together, taking in the beauty of the moment. The tranquility of the beach, combined with the warmth of the sun and the gentle sound of the waves, created a sense of peace that was the perfect ending to their day. As they watched the sun dip below the horizon, they felt a deep sense of connection, both to each other and to the island of St. Lucia.

7. Basseterre, St. Kitts

- **Snorkeling at South Friar's Bay:**

The final island destination of their journey brought the family to St. Kitts, where they began their day with snorkeling at South Friar's Bay. The crystal-clear waters were teeming with life, and the family was eager to explore. The children were especially excited to spot rays and sea turtles, their eyes wide with wonder as they swam alongside these majestic creatures. The coral reefs were vibrant and full of color, and the family marveled at the diversity of the marine life they encountered. The experience was both exhilarating and calming, a perfect start to their day in St. Kitts.

- **Exploring the Rainforest:**

After snorkeling, the family set out to explore the lush rainforests of St. Kitts. The hike took them deep into the heart of the island's natural beauty, with towering trees, exotic plants, and colorful birdlife all around them. The air was filled with the sweet scent of tropical flowers, and the sound of birdsong provided a soothing soundtrack to their hike. As they walked, the family marveled at the diversity of the rainforest, spotting everything from vibrant orchids to playful monkeys swinging through the trees. The hike was a peaceful and rejuvenating experience, a chance to connect with nature and each other.

- **Beachside Picnic at Cockleshell Bay:**

The family's next stop was Cockleshell Bay, a beautiful stretch of sand that provided the perfect setting for a beachside picnic. The meal featured fresh lobster, caught that morning and grilled to perfection, along with a variety of local delicacies. The flavors were fresh and vibrant, a true taste of St. Kitts. As they ate, the family relaxed on the sand, enjoying the warmth of the sun and the gentle breeze coming off the ocean. The meal was a highlight of the day, a chance to savor the flavors of the island while spending quality time together.

- **Final Sunset:**

As the day came to a close, the family gathered on the beach to watch one last sunset. The sky was filled with brilliant colors, and the family sat together, reflecting on the unforgettable experiences they had shared during their island adventures. There was a sense of peace and contentment in the air, as they watched the sun dip below the horizon, casting a golden glow over the ocean. The sunset was a fitting end to their journey, a reminder of the beauty of the world and the importance of family.

The days spent exploring these beautiful islands were perfect, filled with adventure, relaxation, and unforgettable memories. From snorkeling with sea turtles to hiking through lush landscapes, each day allowed the family to reconnect and feel closer than ever. The shared meals, the peaceful sunsets, and the joy of being together in such stunning surroundings left an indelible mark on their hearts. These excursions not only deepened their bonds but also reminded them of the beauty of the world and the importance of family.

Back on the ship, they spent their time indulging in the luxury that surrounded them. There were days when they simply lounged by the pool, sipping cold drinks and basking in the warm sun. The children couldn't get enough of the water slides and ice cream stations, while the adults enjoyed massages at the ship's spa or lost themselves in a good book. Evenings were often spent at the ship's theater, where they watched live performances ranging from Broadway-style musicals to comedy shows that had them all in stitches. Every day was filled with laughter and lightness, each moment a reminder of how special it was to be together.

Intimate Conversations Between Family Members, Strengthening Their Bonds

Amidst all the fun and activities, there were also quieter moments that allowed the family to connect on a deeper level. These intimate conversations, often held during long walks on the deck or over coffee in one of the ship's cozy lounges, gave them the chance to share thoughts and feelings that had been buried under the busyness of life.

Clara and Charlotte, in particular, found themselves having heart-to-heart conversations during their morning walks along the deck. As the ship sailed through the vast ocean, the two women talked about everything—motherhood, marriage, and the challenges they had faced in balancing their careers and families. Charlotte listened with a mother's wisdom, offering advice and encouragement, while Clara expressed her gratitude for the foundation her parents had given her. These moments deepened their bond, bringing them closer as mother and daughter.

Max and Ash, who had always been close as brothers, used the cruise as an opportunity to bond outside work and the restaurant business. Over drinks at the ship's bar or during late-night chats on their balconies, they talked about their relationships, and their hopes for the future. They reminisced about their childhood adventures and discussed their desires to get married. The laughter they shared during these conversations reminded them of the unbreakable bond they had as brothers.

Even the grandchildren had their moments of connection. Eric, the oldest of Clara's children, found himself opening up to his grandfather, Asher, who shared stories of his own childhood and the lessons he had learned along the way. Ginny and Georgia, always full of energy and curiosity, spent hours with their grandmother, Charlotte, asking her about her favorite memories and learning more about their family history. These conversations not only strengthened their relationships but also gave the younger generation a deeper appreciation for their family's roots.

THE IMPORTANCE OF RECONNECTION

As the cruise continued, the family began to reflect on just how important this time together had been. Away from the distractions of everyday life—work, school, and the constant pull of technology—they were able to focus on what truly mattered: their relationships with one another. The ship had become a sanctuary, a place where they could reconnect and rediscover the joy of simply being together.

Reflection on How the Cruise Allowed the Family to Reconnect on a Deeper Level, Free from the Distractions of Everyday Life

Clara, in particular, found herself reflecting on how much she had missed these moments of connection. Her career as a therapist and writer often required her to focus on the problems and emotions of others, but this cruise had allowed her to take a step back and focus on her own family. She realized how much she cherished these bonds, and she made a silent promise to herself to prioritize family time moving forward.

For Max and Ash, the cruise had been a reminder of the importance of balance. Their success in the restaurant industry had brought them both pride and satisfaction, but it had also consumed much of their time and energy. This trip had shown them that there was more to life than work, and that spending time with family was just as valuable as any business achievement. They both felt a renewed sense of purpose, vowing to make more room in their lives for the people they loved.

Charlotte and Asher, who had always been the anchors of the family, felt a deep sense of contentment as they watched their children and grandchildren thrive during the cruise. They had achieved what they had set out to do—they had brought their family back together, creating an environment where love and connection could flourish. As they sat on the deck one evening, watching the sunset hand in hand, they knew that this cruise had been more than just a vacation; it had been a journey of reconnection, healing, and growth.

A Sense of Contentment as They Realize How Much They Mean to Each Other

As the cruise neared its end, the family found themselves filled with a sense of contentment. They had come on this trip with the goal of reconnecting, and they had done just that. The time they had spent together had strengthened their bonds in ways they hadn't anticipated, reminding them of how much they meant to each other.

Each family member felt a renewed sense of love and appreciation for the others, and they knew that the memories they had created on this trip would stay with them for years to come. The laughter, the conversations, the adventures—they were all part of a shared experience that had brought them closer than ever.

The cruise had allowed them to see each other not just as individuals with busy lives, but as a family—a unit that was stronger together. And as they prepared to return to their everyday lives, they carried with them the knowledge that no matter where life took them, they would always have each other. The connection they had rediscovered on this journey would continue to anchor them, reminding them that family was the greatest gift of all.

CHAPTER 6
THE FINAL DAY AT SEA

APPROACHING THE END OF THE CRUISE

The final day of the cruise arrived with a bittersweet feeling in the air. The ship had begun its slow journey back toward the shore, and the familiar sight of land on the horizon brought with it a mix of emotions for the family. As much as they had enjoyed their time together on this floating oasis, the reality of returning to their daily lives was beginning to set in.

The morning was quieter than usual, with everyone taking their time to savor the last few hours on the ship. Charlotte and Asher, always the early risers, were the first to make their way to the deck. They found a secluded spot overlooking the ocean, where the waves gently lapped against the side of the ship.

The sky was painted in soft hues of pink and gold as the sun began to rise, casting a warm glow over the water. They stood there in silence for a moment, taking in the beauty of the morning and the peacefulness that had become a hallmark of their time at sea.

As they watched the horizon slowly inch closer, Charlotte turned to Asher and smiled. "I can't believe it's almost over," she said softly, her voice filled with a mixture of gratitude and longing. Asher nodded in agreement, wrapping his arm around her shoulders. "It's been everything we hoped for and more," he replied. "But I'm not ready to leave just yet."

Soon, the rest of the family began to join them on the deck. Clara arrived with Alexander and the children in tow, the little ones still rubbing the sleep from their eyes as they took in the view. Max and Ash followed not long after, their girlfriends by their sides, all of them carrying cups of coffee and enjoying the cool morning breeze. The group gathered in a loose circle, each of them finding a spot to sit or lean against the railing as they faced the open ocean.

A Mix of Sadness and Gratitude

There was a shared sense of melancholy among them, a quiet understanding that their time on the ship was coming to an end. They had grown so accustomed to the rhythm of cruise life—the lazy mornings, the afternoons of adventure, the evenings filled with laughter—that the thought of returning to their normal routines felt almost surreal. Yet, alongside the sadness was a deep sense of gratitude. This cruise had given them something truly special: the chance to reconnect, to create new memories, and to strengthen the bonds that held them together as a family.

As they sat there, they began to reflect on the highlights of the trip. The children excitedly talked about the fun they'd had at the kids' club, the games they'd played, and the new friends they'd made. Eric, Ginny, and Georgia were already planning to write letters to their new friends once they got home, determined to keep the connections alive even after the cruise ended. Clara and Alexander reminisced about the beautiful destinations they had visited, the peaceful hikes they had taken, and the delicious meals they had enjoyed. Max and Ash joked about their competitive games of mini-golf, each claiming victory despite the fact that neither could agree on who had actually won.

The conversation flowed easily, punctuated by laughter and smiles, as they shared stories of their favorite moments from the trip. Charlotte and Asher listened with full hearts, taking in the joy that radiated from their children and grandchildren. This was exactly what they had hoped for—a chance to bring their family back together, to create lasting memories that would carry them through whatever challenges the future might bring.

A Final Moment Together on the Ship

As the ship continued its journey toward the shore, the family remained on the deck, reluctant to leave their spot. They watched as the coastline grew closer, the details of the land slowly coming into focus. But for now, the ocean still surrounded them, and they wanted to hold on to that feeling of freedom and connection for just a little while longer.

Charlotte suggested that they take a final walk around the ship, a chance to revisit some of the places that had become their favorite spots during the cruise. Together, they made their way around the decks, stopping by the pool where the children had spent hours playing, the theater where they had enjoyed lively performances, and the dining areas where they had shared so many meals. Each stop brought back fond memories, and they took their time, savoring the last moments of their journey.

Eventually, they found themselves back at the spot where they had started the morning—on the top deck, with the ocean stretching out before them. The sun was higher in the sky now, casting a bright light over the water. The air was filled with the sounds of the ship—seagulls calling overhead, the hum of the engines, and the distant chatter of other passengers preparing for their return to shore.

As they gathered once more, Asher took a deep breath and looked out at the horizon. "This has been something special," he said quietly, his voice carrying a note of reflection. "I'm so grateful we had this time together."

The family stood in silence for a moment, letting the weight of Asher's words settle over them. They had all felt the impact of this trip, the way it had brought them closer and reminded them of what truly mattered. There was a sense of peace in knowing that, no matter what challenges lay ahead, they would always have this time—these memories—to hold onto.

With the ship now approaching the shore, the family knew it was time to start preparing for their departure. But before they left the deck, Charlotte suggested one final gesture—a moment of gratitude for the journey they had shared. They joined hands, forming a circle as they stood together. With the ocean as their backdrop, they each took a turn expressing what the trip had meant to them, sharing their gratitude for the time they had spent together.

Clara spoke about how much she had cherished the opportunity to slow down and focus on her family. Max and Ash both expressed their appreciation for the chance to reconnect, not just with their parents and siblings, but with themselves. The children, in their own sweet way, talked about how much fun they had had and how they couldn't wait to do it all over again.

When it was Charlotte's turn, she looked around at her family, her heart full of love. "This cruise has been a gift," she said softly. "A reminder that no matter where life takes us, we'll always have each other. And that's the greatest blessing of all."

With those final words, the family broke their circle and began to make their way back inside, ready to face whatever awaited them onshore. But as they walked away from the deck, they carried with them the peace and connection they had found on this journey, knowing that it would stay with them long after the cruise had ended.

CHAPTER 7

DISEMBARKING AND LOOKING AHEAD

RETURNING TO REALITY

The day had finally arrived for the family to disembark from the cruise ship. After a week of adventure, relaxation, and reconnection, it was time to return to reality. The disembarkation process was a familiar scene of organized chaos—passengers gathering their luggage, saying goodbye to new friends, and shuffling through the busy terminals. But amid the hustle and bustle, the family moved with a calm sense of peace, feeling rejuvenated by the time they had spent together.

As they descended the gangway and set foot on solid ground, the family couldn't help but feel a bittersweet mixture of emotions. On the one hand, there was a sense of sadness that the cruise—their magical escape from everyday life—had come to an end. But on the other hand, they felt closer than ever, having spent the past week reconnecting and strengthening their bonds.

Charlotte and Asher were the first to step off the ship, hand in hand, their expressions filled with contentment. They looked back at the towering cruise ship one last time, silently thanking it for the memories it had given them. Charlotte glanced over at Asher and smiled. "We did it," she said softly, and Asher nodded in agreement. "Yes, we did," he replied. "And it was everything we hoped for."

Behind them, the rest of the family followed, each lost in their own thoughts about the journey they had just experienced. Clara, holding Alexander's hand, watched as her children excitedly talked about their favorite parts of the trip. Eric was still buzzing with excitement about the snorkeling adventures, while Ginny and Georgia couldn't stop talking about the water slides and ice cream stations. Clara smiled at their enthusiasm, feeling grateful for the joy this trip had brought to her family.

Max and Sophie walked together, their luggage rolling behind them, as they talked about how refreshing it had been to step away from the restaurant business for a while. Max was already making plans to bring some of the new recipes he had learned on the cruise into his restaurants, and Sophie was eager to experiment in the kitchen as well. For them, the trip had been both a personal and professional reset.

Ash and Emily brought up the rear, their arms wrapped around each other as they talked about the future. The cruise had given them a chance to reflect on their relationship and their goals, and they felt more aligned than ever. Ash was already thinking about ways to better balance his work life with his personal life, inspired by the quality time they had spent with the family.

As they made their way through the terminal and onto the waiting shuttle, conversations naturally turned to how they would carry the memories and lessons from the cruise into their daily lives. There was an unspoken understanding that this trip had been more than just a vacation—it had been a transformative experience that had redefined their priorities and deepened their relationships.

Clara, always the reflective one, voiced what they were all thinking as they settled into their seats on the shuttle. "I don't want this to end," she said. "Not just the cruise, but the way we've been together. I want to hold on to this feeling, to keep making time for each other, even when life gets busy again."

Her words resonated with everyone, and there were nods of agreement all around. Charlotte and Asher, who had been sitting quietly at the front of the shuttle, turned to face the rest of the family. "We couldn't agree more," Charlotte said. "This trip has reminded us of how important it is to stay connected. We've always known that, but sometimes, life gets in the way. Let's make a promise to each other—to carry this connection forward and not let it slip away again."

A NEW COMMITMENT TO STAYING CONNECTED

The family's conversation on the shuttle soon evolved into a heartfelt discussion about how they could prioritize their relationships moving forward. They began brainstorming ways to stay connected, even as their individual lives pulled them in different directions.

One of the ideas that emerged was the concept of a regular family gathering—a commitment to meet at least once a year for a special trip or a weekend retreat, no matter how busy their schedules became.

They all agreed that it didn't have to be as extravagant as a cruise every time, but it was essential to carve out time when they could all be together, uninterrupted by work or other responsibilities.

Max suggested that they rotate hosting family dinners at their homes, ensuring that even when they weren't traveling, they could still gather around the table and share a meal. Ash added that they should set up a monthly video call, especially for the times when getting together in person wasn't feasible. "No matter where we are," he said, "we should make sure we're staying connected, even if it's just to catch up for an hour."

The children, too, were eager to stay connected with their cousins, Jake and Susan. Eric suggested starting a group chat where they could share photos and stories from their daily lives. Ginny and Georgia chimed in with excitement, already planning their next playdate with their cousins.

As the shuttle made its way to the airport, the family's discussion turned into a joyful planning session, filled with ideas and promises for the future. They were determined to keep the spirit of the cruise alive, to continue creating memories together, and to ensure that the love and connection they had rekindled would carry them forward.

The Love and Connection Rekindled Will Carry Them Forward

By the time they arrived at the airport, the family had made a collective vow—to prioritize their relationships and to never let the busyness of life overshadow what truly mattered. They knew that the cruise was just the beginning of a renewed commitment to each other, a promise to stay connected and continue building on the foundation of love that had always been at the core of their family.

As they hugged each other goodbye at the airport, there was no sadness, only a sense of hope and excitement for what lay ahead. The cruise may have come to an end, but the love and connection they had rediscovered would continue to guide them in the days, months, and years to come.

Charlotte and Asher watched their children and grandchildren walk away, feeling a deep sense of fulfillment. They had achieved what they had set out to do—they had brought their family back together, and in doing so, they had strengthened the bonds that would carry them through whatever life had in store. As they walked hand in hand toward their own gate, Charlotte turned to Asher with a smile. "I think we've started something beautiful," she said.

Asher nodded, his heart full of love for his family. "Yes," he agreed. "And it's only the beginning."

With that, they boarded their flight, ready to face whatever came next, knowing that the love of their family would always be there, anchoring them, no matter where life took them.

CHAPTER 8
CONCLUSION- A LASTING BOND

REFLECTION ON THE JOURNEY

As the family members parted ways after their unforgettable cruise, a quiet reflection settled in each of their hearts. The week they had spent together on the ship felt like a gift—a rare and precious opportunity to reconnect, reflect, and recharge. For Charlotte, it was the culmination of a dream she had held in her heart for a long time—a dream of bringing her family back together in a way that would not just rekindle old bonds but forge new ones that would endure for years to come.

As she sat on the plane next to Asher, looking out at the clouds beneath them, Charlotte couldn't help but reflect on how far they had come as a family. She remembered the early days of raising Clara, Max, and Ash, the joy and the challenges that had come with being a young mother. She remembered the family vacations when the kids were little, the holidays spent gathered around the dinner table, and the countless moments of laughter and love that had defined their lives together.

But she also remembered the recent years, the ones that had felt more fragmented as life pulled them in different directions. The demands of work, school, and the responsibilities of adulthood had slowly chipped away at the time they spent together, creating distance even when the love remained strong. Charlotte had noticed this shift and had felt a quiet ache in her heart, a longing to bring her family back to the closeness they once shared.

The cruise had been her answer to that longing. It had been a bold plan, one that required careful thought, planning, and a leap of faith. But as she looked back on the experience, she knew it had been worth every moment of preparation. The cruise had given them the chance to reconnect on a deeper level, to remind themselves of what truly mattered: family, love, and the bonds that could never be broken.

Charlotte's dream of bringing her family back together had been fulfilled, and the experience had left a lasting impact on everyone. Each family member had come away from the trip with a renewed sense of purpose and connection. They had rediscovered the joy of being together, free from the distractions of their daily lives, and in doing so, they had strengthened the foundation of their family.

For Clara, the cruise had been a reminder of how much she valued her family's support, especially as she balanced her career and motherhood. Max and Ash had found new ways to connect with each other, not just as brothers but as friends and business partners who could lean on one another for support. Even the children had come away with a deeper appreciation for the family ties that connected them, having created memories with their cousins that they would treasure forever.

As they all returned to their respective homes and resumed their daily routines, they carried with them the lessons and memories of the cruise. The experience had been a powerful reminder that no matter where life took them, their family would always be their anchor, their safe harbor in a world that could sometimes feel overwhelming.

AN ENDURING LOVE

As the days turned into weeks and the weeks into months, the family began to settle back into the rhythm of their everyday lives. But the love and connection they had rekindled on the cruise remained with them, like a warm glow that never faded. They kept their promise to stay connected, making time for regular family gatherings, dinners, and video calls. Each time they came together, they felt the bond that had been strengthened during the cruise—a bond that was now unbreakable.

For Charlotte and Asher, the cruise had given them something priceless: the knowledge that their family was closer than ever, that the love they had nurtured over the years had only grown stronger with time. They watched with pride as their children and grand-children carried forward the lessons of love, connec-tion, and family that they had worked so hard to instill.

The memories of the cruise became a touchstone for the family, a reminder of the bond that held them together. Whether they were gathered around a dinner table, sharing stories from their lives, or simply enjoying a quiet moment together, they knew that the love and support of their family would always be there, no matter where life took them.

Years later, as they looked back on the cruise, the family would realize that it had been more than just a vacation—it had been a transformative experience that had deepened their relationships and left them with memories they would cherish forever. The laughter, the conversations, the adventures—they were all part of a shared history that had brought them closer, that had reminded them of the strength of their bond.

That bond, forged in love and strengthened by time, would endure for years to come. It would carry them through the challenges of life, the moments of joy and sorrow, the milestones, and the everyday moments. And as they continued to grow, as their lives took them in new directions, they would always know that they had each other—family, love, and a connection that could never be broken.

As they parted ways after the cruise, they did so not with sadness but with a sense of hope and excitement for the future. They knew that the journey they had shared on the ship was just the beginning of a new chapter in their lives—a chapter filled with love, connection, and the promise of more adventures together. The cruise may have ended, but the bond they had rediscovered would last a lifetime.

The End

ABOUT THE AUTHORS

Maria-Claire Moriah Wright is a hard-working and ambitious teenager currently navigating the exciting world of 10th grade. Driven by a passion for both writing and helping others, Maria-Claire aspires to one day become a writer and therapist—a unique combination that reflects her deep empathy and love for storytelling. With her eyes set on a future where she can make a difference in people's lives through her words and guidance, she approaches each day with determination and purpose.

Beyond her academic pursuits, Maria-Claire is a loving child who cherishes the connections she has with those around her. She values the importance of good friendships and believes in nurturing relationships that are built on trust, kindness, and mutual support. Her warm and open-hearted nature makes her a cherished friend, and she finds joy in sharing meaningful conversations and laughter with those she holds dear.

An expressive soul, Maria-Claire has a passion for dancing. Whether she's moving to the rhythm of her favorite music or losing herself in the flow of a routine, dance allows her to express her creativity and connect with her inner self. It's a form of expression that brings her happiness and adds a sense of grace and balance to her life.

Maria-Claire also has a love for travel and exploring new places. She finds excitement in discovering different cultures, tasting new foods, and experiencing the beauty of the world around her. Nature is a source of peace and inspiration for Maria-Claire, and she delights in spending time outdoors, whether it's hiking through lush forests, relaxing on a beach, or simply enjoying the fresh air.

Swimming is another one of her passions. The feeling of being in the water gives her a sense of freedom and serenity, allowing her to escape the stresses of daily life and embrace the beauty of the present moment. Whether she's swimming in a calm lake or diving into the ocean's waves, Maria-Claire finds a deep connection with nature through the water.

With her dreams, kindness, and adventurous spirit, Maria-Claire Moriah Wright is on a path to creating a future where she can combine her love for writing, therapy, and human connection. She is a shining example of a young person who understands the importance of balancing ambition with the joy of living in the moment, and she is sure to inspire others along the way.

David Saccoh Wright is a hard-working professional whose dedication to global peace, security, and development has made a lasting impact through his work at the United Nations. His efforts focus on supporting key initiatives for Africa, a continent he is deeply passionate about. David's work revolves around promoting good governance, the rule of law, and sustainable development across African nations, contributing to a vision of a peaceful and prosperous future for all.

Driven by his commitment to positive change, David has also turned to the power of the written word to inspire and guide the next generation. Through his poetry, he encourages African youth to look to the heroes and leaders of the past, drawing lessons from their courage and wisdom. His writings serve as a call to action for young people to become good citizens and role models, shaping a brighter future by embodying the principles of leadership and integrity.

David's faith is central to his life, and he is a deeply God-fearing man who finds spiritual fulfillment in his study and writing about the Bible. His reflections on scriptures from both the Old and New Testaments highlight the timeless messages of faith, love, and redemption. At the heart of his spiritual writings is the central figure of Jesus Christ, whom David reveres as the Savior and Redeemer. Through his work, he draws others closer to the teachings of Christ, offering spiritual guidance and insight.

In addition to his professional and spiritual pursuits, David has a love for travel and a deep appreciation for nature. He enjoys exploring new places, finding joy in discovering the beauty and diversity of the world. Whether he is hiking through scenic landscapes or simply enjoying moments of peace and tranquility in nature, David values the sense of calm and renewal that comes from connecting with the natural world.

David Saccoh Wright's life is a testament to his dedication to service, both in his work for peace and development in Africa and in his spiritual writings. He continues to inspire those around him, guiding others with his passion for good governance, faith, and the beauty of life's simple pleasures.